Moon Cycle Intention Journal
2021

ISBN 978-1-7774461-0-9

ToolsForTransformation.ca

Our intention for this book

Moon Cycle Intention Journal offers a sacred container within which you can practise a return to your natural cycles with the Moon as companion. Access the positive supportive feedback that validates your own inner wisdom experiences and joyfully explore your intuitive knowing as it invites personal discovery and a fuller integration of feminine energies into your everyday life.

"There is a moon inside every human being. Learn to be companions with it."

Rumi

Contents

WELCOME

" Let the waters settle and you will see the moon and the stars mirrored in your own being."

Rumi

Welcome!

We're so glad you're here.

And we're so honoured to share this Journal with you. This book, first and foremost, is a labour of love. We cooked up a plan to share our Moon wisdom tools, build a thing of beauty, and have a whole lot of fun doing it. And voila! The *Moon Cycle Intention Journal* was born.

This book is designed as a stand-alone tool to support you on your personal journey into yourself. Before we even started the first page, as is the way of a powerful intention-setting practice, we crafted and sat with our intentions for it.

It is important for us to create and offer it with joy and ease. We want our inspiration in working and playing with these tools over the years to come through and feel inspiring for you. This *Moon Cycle Intention Journal* was conceived as an uplifting and above all practical tool, supporting a rich reconnection with your own deep feminine knowingness as a manifested presence on our planet.

The only piece of this puzzle that's needed now is you.

Turn the page, commit to your opening, and let's begin...

With infinite joy,

Valanne & Sasha

How To Use This Journal

When we set out to design your *Moon Cycle Intention Journal*, naturally we set many intentions for its beauty, desirability and popularity, as well as for the pure enjoyment of making it! But our primary intention was always for its usefulness: this is a book that wants to be used.

This section is where you'll discover how to make the best use of this *Journal* and all the ways it supports you to reconnect with your deep feminine knowingness using the cycles of the Moon.

Keep in mind that the very nature of feminine energy is its changeability. These guidelines are just suggestions: possible ways to see, feel and experience the Moon you're in. Consider them only as prompts to help you explore more deeply. Ultimately, setting intentions is a totally personal experience, a dance between you and your deepest desires resulting in statements that support you to take inspired action.

Setting Your Intentions

Moon Cycle Intention Journal is first and foremost designed to support your powerful intention-setting practice. Already have an established intention-setting practice? Great! You may choose to read over *Holding Space For Manifestation* (pg 20) as review. And you may find some helpful tips going forward.

If you're just starting out, you'll want to read all of *Holding Space For Manifestation* to get a good handle on what's what in the realm of intention-setting. It isn't complicated but, like any practice, it has unique aspects that are helpful to know.

Choosing Moon Cycles

Six Months: You may choose to set your intentions using the six-month cycle from New Moon to Full Moon in the same sign. This cycle is used for bigger picture or medium-term intentions. An intention you set during the Scorpio New Moon in November may come to full fruition at the Scorpio Full Moon in May of the following year.

One Month: You may also choose to use this Journal to set short-term intentions within a one-month Moon Cycle. For instance, you can use the Full Moon to reflect on the qualities and efficacy of your intention set during the New Moon two weeks earlier.

NEW MOON JOURNAL PAGE

The *New Moon Journal Page* has sections to serve your intention-setting practice by introducing various layers of expression, meaning and symbolism to each month's New Moon based on the sign it's in.

TITLE

The page title tells you what sign the New Moon is in. The calendar date and time of the New Moon in Eastern Time is at the top of the opposing page.

ELEMENT

The 12 Astrological signs are each assigned one of the four elements: fire, air, water and earth. The qualities of these elements describe the energies of the sign with which they're associated. These attributes help you feel into the essential nature of the elemental energies at play on any given New Moon. This knowledge can support you by pointing you in a particular direction as you contemplate your desires and your intention statement.

Fire: **Aries, Leo, Sagittarius** – active, energetic, passionate, daring, courageous, assertive, inspired, impulsive, volatile, spirited

Air: **Gemini, Libra, Aquarius** – logical, intellectual, mental, rational, objective, conceptual, curious, communicative, social, detached

Water: Cancer, Scorpio, Pisces – receptive, sensitive, empathic, emotional, ungrounded, compassionate, subjective, fluid,"soulful"

Earth: Taurus, Virgo, Capricorn – practical, stable, consistent, methodical, reliable, patient, grounded, sensual, cautious, rigid

EXPRESSION

The 12 Astrological signs are each assigned one of two *Expressions*: Feminine or Masculine. Rather than having to do with gender, this desigation speaks of Yin or Yang energy held within the sign. Yin or feminine energy is typically having to do with dark, receptive, nighttime, cool, quiet, fluid, flexible, powerful, potential. Yang or masculine energy is associated with active, bright, hot, daytime, forceful, strong, spark, upward movement.

Knowing what *Expression* and *Element* are present during each New Moon can help inform your intention-setting each month. Take time to feel into all the underlying energies of each sign the New Moon is moving through as you shape your intention.

ESSENCE

Each Moon sign's *Essence* represents its underlying energetic theme. In a way, all the other keywords associated with that astrological sign move in tandem with its essential nature. For example, *Capricorn's Essence* is "I Use": it wants to build, create and manifest concrete things in the world.

NOBLE QUALITIES

These keywords represent the aspirational side of the Moon sign. Reviewing them you may only feel attracted to one or two, or you may recognize many as feeling relevant for you during this New Moon phase. Though we've typically chosen classic representations of the most positive qualities of each sign, don't feel shy about researching your own, or considering the various meanings and synonyms for each quality. The key here is to sense into how each word makes you *feel*, not necessarily what your brain thinks is correct or appropriate.

SHADOW SIDE

Like the Moon herself, every sign has a 'dark' side – versions of its expression that are more difficult, less helpful, and sometimes downright ugly to deal with. These shadow aspects can also be tricky because they tend to hide out…in the dark! The best way to deal with a shadow? Begin by watching for it. Without judgement. Some persistent but gentle observation goes a long way to uncovering the less attractive qualities of any sign, and ultimately transforming them into something constructive.

NEW MOON FOCUS

In this section we offer you eight possible access points into the energies of the New Moon that may prompt intention statements for you. As with the *Noble Qualities*, you may only feel attracted to one or two, or you may recognize many as feeling relevant for you during this New Moon phase. Allow yourself to ponder each statement and sit with how it feels in the moment. Is there a natural resonance? Does one statement really stand out or 'ring true' for you? Perhaps only part of one or more of the focus statements speaks to you. There is no right or wrong here. Follow your intuition. After all, that's what playing with the Moon is all about!

AFFIRMATION

Each sample affirmation on the *New Moon Journal* page is one you may wish to use during meditation or visualization, or you may wish to post it somewhere you can easily see it during the Moon cycle to which it belongs. You may also like to reframe it into a somewhat related but different affirmation that works better for you at this time.

NEW MOON INTENTION PAGE

This lined, note-book style page is designed to serve your intention-setting practice by offering you the opportunity to craft your personal intention statements in a definitive way that enables you to regularly revisit them. Also, this page encourages you to note or journal your observations throughout the month or six months following your intention.

If you're just starting out, you'll want to read the *Holding Space for Manifestation* (pg 20) and *How to Craft an Intention* (pg 22) sections in order to get a good idea of how to write a powerful intention statement.

LISTEN

A key element of intention-setting is paying attention to what happens *after* you set your intention and craft your clear, positive statement. Remember: you are partnering with universal energy to manifest your biggest dreams and deepest desires. Together you are *co-creating* your reality and an important part of any relationship is communication, which is a two-way street.

So, once you've expressed what you need to say by way of your intention statement, your job is to be a good partner by listening with care. Practise listening with all your senses.

WATCH FOR SIGNS

Set your internal system to be alert to synchronicity. So often stuff shows up and we ignore, deny or otherwise miss it. Our culture tends to reward the big, loud, noisy wins or only acknowledge obvious "aha" moments. Not only are we not primed to hear, see or feel what is more understated or refined, we're often taught to dismiss it as irrelevant.

Universal energy, and particularly Moon energy, is subjective and subtle. Feedback letting you know you're on the right track might show up as 'out of the blue' experiences, seemingly random thoughts or ideas, pictures in your imagination, messages in song lyrics, dreams, physical tingling or change of body temperature, sudden knowing, repeated words, phrases or numerical series, and more.

Be open to noticing. Be receptive to the magic that's all around you. Use the *Synchronicity Pages* at the back of this book to help you take note of, track and refer back to your observations, experiences and awarenesses.

TAKE INSPIRED ACTION

Intention-setting is a fluid and flexible process. Results will likely fall on a spectrum of experience. By maintaining alert attention to the daily energy flow around you while holding your intention gently but firmly in your awareness, you can stay open to the opportunities that arise to take inspired action. Staying relaxed but attentive is a practice that enables you to take utmost advantage of what each moment's energy is offering.

If you are working with a short-term intention within a one-month Moon cycle, you may have fewer, bigger steps to take to fulfill your dream. Working within a longer, six-month Moon cycle, your initial actions in the early part of the intention cycle may be minimal, respecting the gestational nature of the New Moon's energy.

FULL MOON JOURNAL PAGE

This page has sections to serve your intention-setting practice by introducing opportunities for reflection on the intention you set during the previous New Moon (either two weeks or six months earlier). The keywords and phrases for the sign of each month's Full Moon are meant as prompts to help illuminate all the aspects of your existing intention and prepare it for review and revision.

TITLE

The page title at the top tells you what sign the Full Moon is in, with the calendar date and time in Eastern Time at the top of the opposing page.

REFLECTION

Intention is feminine, fluid and flexible by nature. This makes pairing it with the Moon cycles a perfect friendship. The Full Moon phase, with the height of the Moon's illumination as it faces the Sun, is the ideal time to review all your intention statements. Reassess, reconsider and revise wherever the current Full Moon energies prompt you.

Asking good, open-ended questions is a foundational part of any resilient intention practice. Using basic assessment questions during the Full Moon is an excellent way to unearth any hidden dissonance, weakness or potential drawbacks to your intention. These include:

What's working? What isn't working? What needs to change?

This is a good time for minor course corrections, a complete overhaul or even the abandonment of intentions that may no longer feel aligned with your deeper knowingness once the spotlight of the Full Moon shines its light on them. What is revealed may be an intention that is derived more from expectations you have of yourself or perceive others have of you, rather than your true heart's desire. Be honest without harshness and you'll find your way to helpful revisions that yield much more meaningful results for you in the end.

HIGHER EXPRESSION

Like the *Noble Qualities* of the New Moon sign, these keywords represent how the Full Moon best shows up when it is moving through a sign. Reviewing them you may only feel attracted to one or two, or you may recognize many as feeling relevant for you during this Full Moon phase. Though we've typically chosen classic representations of the positive expressions of each sign, feel free to seek out your own. Most importantly, notice how each word makes you *feel*, rather than focusing on its dictionary definition.

LOWER EXPRESSION

We all slip into a lesser, not so desirable version of ourselves on occasion. These "lower expressions" can be difficult, frustrating or downright awful to deal with. The best thing about having these energies show up during a Full Moon is that, unlike during the dark of the New Moon, everything is illuminated! It's so much easier to see what's going on under the bright light of this Full Moon phase. So just be willing to see what is arising, watch for it without judgement, and use your newfound awareness to make the shifts you need to bring your intention into greater alignment with its highest version.

Make good use of the *Higher Expression* attributes by considering how you can invite more of what you want into your life to balance what you want less of (the *Lower Expression*). For instance, if during the Gemini Full Moon you notice yourself over-thinking an intention and getting stuck in your head about how you really feel, call on Gemini's super powers of communication, sociability and versatility. Articulate the problem to a friend and be open-minded as you allow the innovative solutions to flow to you.

See the *Shift* section of each Full Moon page for examples.

LIKES

These keywords and phrases can act as prompts to what is most attractive about the energies of this particular Full Moon: that which is appealing, pleasant desirable.

DISLIKES

These keywords and phrases can act as prompts to what is least attractive about the energies of this particular Full Moon: that which is repellent, disagreeable, unwelcome.

SHIFT

This section celebrates the dynamic nature of Moon energies – their variability and innate capacity to transform something that feels heavy, problematic or oppressive into something more beneficial, uplifting and expansive.

DESIRES

The Moon Energy *Desires* represent underlying themes for each Full Moon sign. Try speaking them out loud and notice how each one makes you feel. Does it help you connect with the energies of its Full Moon sign?

FULL MOON REFLECTION PAGE

This lined, note-book style page is designed to serve your intention-setting practice by offering you the opportunity to reflect on and revise your personal intention statements. This is the ideal place to note or journal about all your fears, questions or concerns regarding your intentions.

This phase is typically a time of fruition or manifestation. It's the period when natural flaws in your plan will reveal themselves most readily. Use the dominant energies of whatever sign this Full Moon is in to inform your overall intention-setting practice and revamp those intentions that aren't fully aligned with what you truly want.

Take this time for self-acknowledgement, celebrate your successes, and recognize your achievements, no matter how small.

VOID OF COURSE MOON SECTION

The Moon's void of course period is a lovely timing tool you can use to support your intention-setting practice. As the Moon progresses through her phases, she moves in and out of astrological signs, such as Scorpio, encountering relationships with other planets along the way. These relationships are known as 'aspects'. At some point just before moving out of one sign and into the next, the Moon will be entirely free of aspects. She glides through the sky unencumbered by any relationships to other celestial bodies or their energies.

This void of course time can last seconds, minutes or hours and can feel open-ended, ungrounded, formless. Though it's an ideal time to meditate, dream, imagine, rest or retreat, it is best to avoid anything that requires definitive action or follow-up. Use any void of course time to feel into the energies surrounding your intention or reflection, but try not to make definitive decisions or take action for your intention until the Moon has moved out of her void of course and into her next sign.

Void of Course Avoids: Initiate communications seeking a response; start a new job, business or project; have a meeting that generates action items; make investments or open accounts; deal with clients; get married; sign contracts, etc. Use the void of course schedule provided on page 96.

ASTROLOGICAL HOUSES PAGES

Each of your *Journal* pages throughout the year is dedicated to the sign the New or Full Moon finds herself in each month.

In your astrological chart*, which is a symbolic map of the sky, each sign falls into a particular house or section. These 12 pie-shaped divisions or houses represent different areas of your life experience. e.g. the first is the house of the self, the second is the house of material possessions, etc.

The house pages at the end of this *Journal* (pg 86) contain details for each of these themes. The themes describe the life arenas in which the Moon energies will play out for you. This is where the Moon's energies are brought down to earth. It's within your house themes that intention-setting gets up close and personal: here you can address your day-to-day concerns directly with your intention statements.

With the Scorpio New Moon for instance, check your chart to see what house Scorpio is in. That tells you what theme the Scorpio New Moon is impacting for you. This perspective adds another layer of energy to your intention-setting, supporting you to craft intentions that help you live your best life forward.

The signs and houses in your chart never change, only the planets moving through them. The Moon is the quickest of all celestial bodies, making her way through each sign in about 2 1/2 days.

For a free copy of your *Whole Sign natal chart go to astro.com.

SYNCHRONICITY NOTES PAGES

You might think of synchronicity as an amusing coincidence, a kind of quirky happenstance randomly occurring in an otherwise routine day. Whether or not you find it entertaining however, synchronicity actually plays a key role in developing a powerful intention-setting practice.

Synchronicity generally refers to simultaneous experiences which seem related yet have no apparent 'causal connection'. But the very act of setting an intention is itself a conscious act of co-creation. By following the steps to craft a clear intention statement which leads to inspired action, *you become* the causal connection. Your focus, your passion, your intention – these are what makes a 'fluke' potentially relevant.

Within the scope of intention-setting, you and your heart's desire are at the centre. So, when synchronicity shows up, ask yourself, "Is this meaningful to me?" If the connection touches you, then you are matching your frequency with the universal flow. You are literally synchronizing your own energy with your desired outcome. With practice, synchronicity expands.

Because as we know, where your attention goes, energy flows.

Use the *Synchronicity Pages* at the back of this book to help you take note of, track and refer back to your observations, experiences and awarenesses. You may be amazed at what you find.

MANIFESTATION

Holding Space for Manifestation

Steps for Setting Powerful Intentions

Intention-setting is part of an energetic dance. This is the dance of co-creation. Its steps include holding a clear, unencumbered space within you for the possibility of manifesting your dreams and desires. The better defined the path and choreography, the easier the process. Powerful intentions are like trees: they emerge from rich soil, rooted deep beneath the surface, rising up to bear fruit. They need strong roots. To have intentions bear fruit you must first 'nurture the soil'. This includes clearing undesirable blocking beliefs that entangle and slow their growth.

The feminine energy that holds space for the intention to be seeded is your *attitude*. This is your personal perspective or How You Show Up for yourself and your sacred dream. Though your intention may have been inspired by external wants or needs, its growth and development begins within.

Like any dance, learning to finesse the steps takes some practice. Unlike repeating soccer drills or piano scales, this routine is meant to be approached with an attitude of curiosity and joy. Try different things. See what works. Ultimately, establish a practice of sitting quietly with each intention statement for 8-10 minutes. (see *How to Set an Intention* pg 23)

1

Intention energy needs a clear space to expand

Maintain an attitude of open-hearted acceptance

- Be receptive; foster flexibility and allowing
- Release expectation, judgement, attachment
- **Remember:** Your intention result may not look the way you think it should

Setting potent intentions is a heart-centred practice. A key to producing powerful results is to allow yourself to move out of your head and into your heart. Practice quietening your thinking mind and instead sink into a felt sense of gratitude, joy or love.

2

Intention energy is naturally magnetic

Set and hold a positive tone

- Always craft your intention with the language of what you DO want ~ It may be easy for you to begin by thinking about what you don't want, and then focus on the positive
- Make your statements helpful, supportive, constructive
- **Remember:** What you focus on expands

The overall tone of the intention statement must be positive. It always seeks the best or highest outcome for all parties involved, no matter what your subjective feelings or opinions may be.

3

Intention energy wants clear direction

Refine your intention statement with definite timing

- State your intention in present tense – as if what you desire already exists
- Make it persistent – consistent, constant, lasting
- **Remember:** The natural fluidity of intention needs parameters

Because the nature of intention energy is fluid, it needs boundaries. Think of it as setting parameters around a source of infinite abundance. Because universal energy can take any form, it's helpful to specify what you want it to be without making the limits so restrictive that the flow of possibility is prevented.

4

Intention energy requires that you remain open

Be grounded and alert to opportunities to step into Inspired Action

- Maintain a trusting heart, clear mind & relaxed body in the spirit of surrender
- Embrace your ability to take steps toward your desired outcome
- **Remember:** You are an empowered co-creator partnered with an infinitely abundant, benevolent universe

Notice how much attention is placed on 'how' you show up for your intention as compared to what action you take to 'make something happen'. Rather than force or push, stay grounded and allow opportunities to flow toward you. Then each action you take becomes inspired rather than careless or haphazard. When you are open-hearted and relaxed, going with the flow of 'what is', you are naturally aligned with universal energy, fully supporting the fruition of your intention.

How To Craft an Intention

FOSTERING INTENTIONAL LANGUAGE

Speaking the language of intention really makes the difference between wishful hoping and manifesting with clarity and precision

Be attentive to the language you use when setting intentions. Language is powerful magic. Think in terms of incantations and the way they hold the energy of your intention. Always choose supportive, positive, win/win language when crafting your intentions.

Supportive Language	**Unsupportive Language**
Abundant	Get Better
Complete	Will Improve
Consistent	Less of ___
Free	Must have
Happy	Sometime
Healthy	Wish / Hope

Intentional language can also act as a tool to help you seek out and shift negative language patterns that stem from blocking beliefs. These beliefs typically come from cultural or familial expectations rather than from your own inner wisdom. A good adage to consider is to not 'believe everything you think'.

Beware of your various blocking belief statements – use your powers of observation to watch for these types of phrases in your speech or self-talk. Never use them within your intention statements.

I can't	Life doesn't work that way
It never	Definitely / Absolutely
They always	It's so unfair
That's how I am	I'm not ___ enough

Once you've devised a draft intention statement, step away from it for a little while, even just a few minutes. When you return, ask yourself these questions:

? ***How does my intention statement make me feel?***

? ***Does my intention statement land with authority or feel ungrounded?***

? ***Am I practicing self-doubt or cultivating self-trust with this intention statement?***

HOW TO SET AN INTENTION

This section could really be called: *How to Establish a Powerful Intention-setting Practice.* Like repeating a particular set of dance steps, the more often we replicate the same pattern in our intention practice, the more easily we internalize the choreography. Until suddenly the steps have become second nature, part of our body knowing.

This co-creative dance we're in is a partnership with universal life force. Our role is to regularly show-up with an open heart ready to receive. This sounds super simple but can be quite challenging. After all, life's demands can easily get in the way. Holding a sacred space for yourself to regularly engage with intention-setting is vital to the success of the process.

Set the Stage

Whether or not you are sensitive to your surroundings, the space you're in does impact you. Consider intention-setting like any other meditative or mindfulness-based practice. Begin by supporting your five senses in ways that feel calming and promote inner connection.

Ask yourself:

- What smells appeal? You may wish to burn herbs, diffuse essential oils, etc.
- What sights help me focus? You may like to burn a candle, focus on a mandala, etc.
- What sounds calm me? You may prefer meditative music, chanting or silence.
- What tastes good? You may enjoy a warm, soothing drink beforehand.
- What feels familiar? You may prefer the same chair, cushion, blanket or shawl.

Any or all of these things help you to raise your frequency and become more receptive to the process of intention-setting.

Signal the Energy Shift

Crafting powerful intentions comes in part from developing a strong intention-setting practice. As with any routine, repetition yields mastery. Regularly setting a specific time, sitting in the same spot, facing the same direction, using the same pillow, shawl, etc., all triggers cellular memory. When we signal the inner perceptions with outer actions it becomes increasingly easier to move into that receptive frame of reference we need to experience effective intention-setting.

Come from Your Heart

In our left-brain world academic thinking and scientific knowledge tend to take precedence over intuition and heart-based feeling. With intention-setting it can be helpful to practice getting out of your own way. Remember that the mind is designed to be receptive: like a parachute, it 'functions best when open'.

Using any heart-centering practice will enable you to maintain heart-centred focus throughout the time you sit with your intention. Once you feel well-connected into your heart space, say the intention statement out loud. Think of it like an incantation that brings weight to the statement.

Allow Yourself to Drop into You

Going within sounds simple. And in fact, it is. But it can also be difficult. Moving into yourself isn't something our culture reinforces. Most parents didn't model it, school doesn't teach it, and our hectic adult lifestyle discourages it.

So, be patient with yourself. Let go of all your expectations. Move into a state of *allowing*. Be curious and alert. Soften and become the gentle observer without judgement. Open to the possibilities of what 'comes to you'. Notice sensations, images, feelings, sounds, memories, etc. Trust what you 'get'.

Distracted? That's ok. Call yourself back to the loving feeling in your heart. Remember: There's no wrong way

Make it a Habit

Any good practice requires just that, practice. Establish the steps that work best for you.

Once you have crafted your intention statement, set the stage and dropped into your heart, read your statement out loud. Observe what you see, hear, feel. Just notice. Journal any observations.

Intention Examples

My intention *is that I consistently experience easy flow and connection to creative source in all my writing under all conditions with grace and ease, in greatest good for all.*

My intention *is that I have healed the root cause of all inflammation and its manifestations and all cells have returned to their optimal order in highest health and greatest good for all.*

My intention *is that my sales register a tenfold increase 6 months from today.*

WHAT INTENTION ISN'T...

➢ A Goal

A goal is typically something we move toward. In the game of hockey for instance, the focus is to 'score a goal' by maneuvering the puck into the opponent's net. Though goal-setting serves a purpose in many environments, it is best engaged *after* the intention steps have been initiated. Goal-setting is essentially a masculine energy, linear in nature and primarily concerned with taking specific actions to attain an end result.

➢ Wishful Hoping

Wishful hoping is a state of mind and heart that can be characterized by lack of clarity and lack of commitment. It is a convenient way to daydream or maintain a non-committal position on a situation or relationship you may enjoy imagining but, whether out of fear, unworthiness, etc., you cannot truly feel or embody within yourself.

➢ Focused on Action

Action is the part of intention-setting that we call *approach.* Our culture typically focuses on implementation in the form of planning, list-making, strategizing or problem-solving. However, this is only one piece of the intention-setting puzzle, usually *the last one.*

➢ Fixed in Time/Space

An intention is essentially a frequency. And it takes some practice to be able to hold space for the energy of an intention. Because we've been trained since childhood to only value what we can see, it can seem strange or confusing to entrust our dream to something not fixed in time and space that we cannot touch or measure.

Meet the Moon

Within you there resides a Moon. She is ever changing, yet as steadfast as the seasons.

She beckons you to come closer so she can whisper secrets, intimacies and deep knowing about what you truly want and how you wish to walk in the world, that only you can hear. This inner Moon is your muse, a source of inspiration and illumination, lighting your path forward on your personal journey. She encourages you to sing your soul's song with conviction, to dance wildly or demurely as you feel called to do, and above all to dream your heart's deepest desires into being.

Your personal, expressive, hidden inner Moon loves to dance, sing and cavort with the Moon in the sky. As she makes her way across the sky each cycle, this Moon's many faces shine out brightly and then fade to black. She is the one we see daily or nightly, the one who rules the ocean tides, the planting and harvesting timetable, the rhythmic ebb and flow of our daily energetic climate.

This Moon makes no light of her own. She is by nature relational, reflective of whatever pervasive energy she's in. The part of her that is always dark or hidden from view is symbolic of your inner psyche, encouraging pensive introspection. She rules over your vulnerability, inner complexity and how you receive support from others. She is subjective and irrational, governing your originality and intuition. Her changeability encourages the development of new habits while her fluidity allows you to align with the current of universal co-creative energy in your unique ways. The Moon can represent your inner healer, responsible for keeping you open and loving; your inner mother, whose job it is to keep you emotionally fed and secure; or your inner visionary, capable of imagining your biggest and best dreams.

The natural flow of this Moon energy not only informs your day-to-day choices and movements, but helps you intend your future forward.

This *Journal* is your personal invitation to enter into a sacred relationship with this natural feminine energy flow. Catch the energies of the New Moon to craft rich, powerful intentions and use the Full Moon reflection phase to celebrate your gains and review, revise and renew your commitment to your wildest dreams and deepest desires.

The Phases of the Moon

The Moon shows us her new face every day – her individual character as she moves through the sky. Her innate changeability supports us in gaining fresh perspective, setting a new tone for a project or establishing new habits. The Moon's many phases describe her relationship to the Sun, the flow of energy between our intuitive awareness (Moon) and our conscious viewpoint (Sun). From the perspective of our natural world, the life cycle of a fruiting tree is a beautiful metaphor for the Moon phase cycle. Each phase symbolizes the growth cycle from seed to blossom, fruit to dormancy: life, growth, zenith, deterioration, death, rebirth. In turn, each of those stages may invite intention, reflection, dissemination or integration. Each phase ushers in a set of energies like a wave we can ride to support the realisation of our dreams and desires going forward.

In this *Journal* we focus on the New Moon phase for crafting intentions and the Full Moon phase for reviewing and revising those intentions.

NEW MOON PHASE = Seed Sowing

This is the portal before the true beginning, when the Sun and Moon are in the same astrological sign, bringing extra power to the energies of that sign. A dark, quiet, empty time of pure potential, use it to set intentions, initiate relationships, contemplate an idea, outline a new project, plant seeds and unfold into your more authentic, timeless self. This can be an ideal time to go within, access a deeper level of guidance, consider carefully what you most wish to cultivate in yourself and your life, and remember who you really are. Lay the groundwork for manifestation and then tend it for six months.

The planted seed holds the blueprint of possibility for the mature plant. The full plant potential – all it can be – lives within the seed. Tending to soil quality and planting at the right time is key. This is the phase that fosters our complete trust within the darkness of unrealised potential.

FULL MOON = Harvest

Here the Moon acts as an illuminating cosmic spotlight. She is directly opposite the Sun in the sky, fully reflecting its powerful light. This opposition offers a greater amplification of our vision and potential, bringing awareness to our outer-world ego and its various manifestations. This is also a time of peak clarity, pointing the way to an alternate perspective we may not otherwise have considered. It can be an opportunity to shine a light on your 'shadow', those parts of you or your life that feel shameful, messy or unrefined that you tend to hide, deny or ignore. It's also a time to celebrate your growth and assess your progress, making necessary course corrections on the road ahead. Reap what you have intended six months earlier.

This is the peak point of growth for the tree. It is a time of fulfillment with an acute awareness of the shift in the cycle away from expansion.

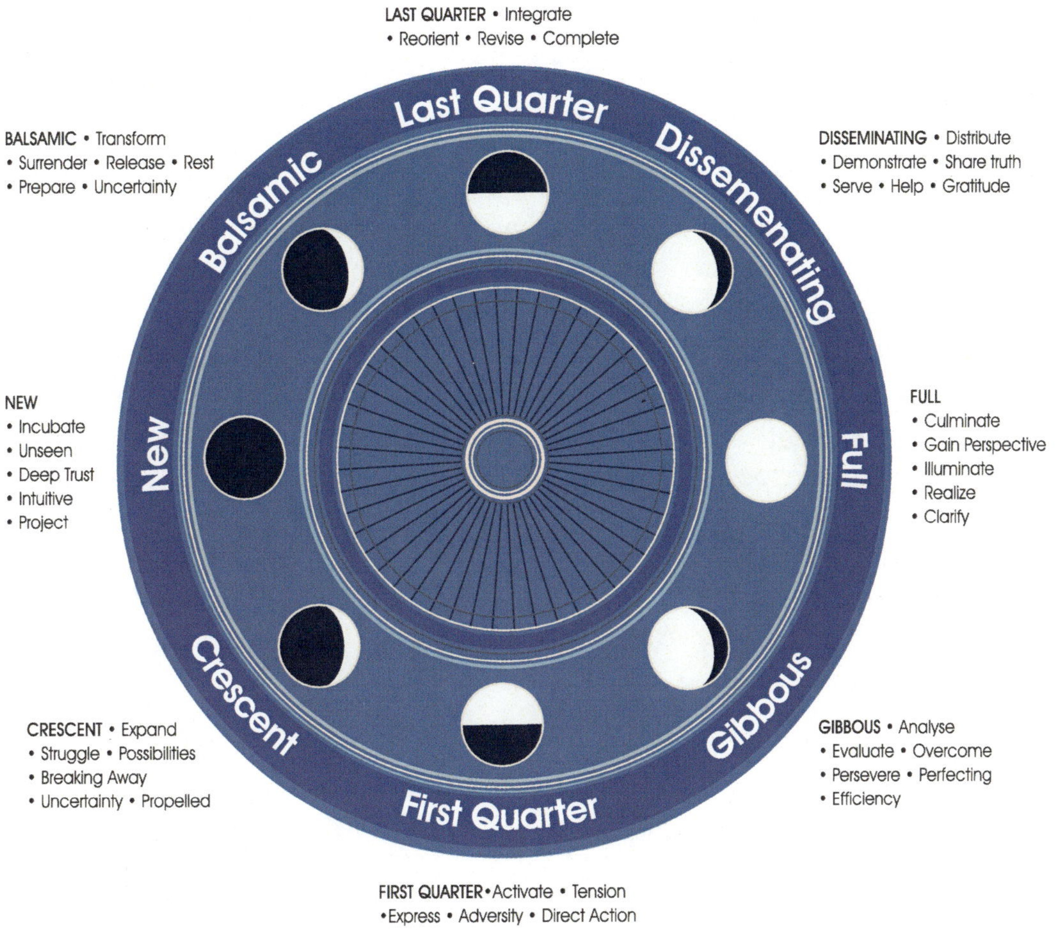

Scorpio New Moon

Element: Water
Expression: Feminine
Symbol: Scorpion

ESSENCE: I DESIRE

Noble Qualities: Transcendent, evolutionary, enlightened, magic, passionate, profound, spiritual, sensitive, intuitive, visionary, shamanic, investigative, intimate, surrendering, mysterious, mystical, intense

Shadow Side: Secretive, jealous, paranoid, over-sensitive, relentless, resentful, crisis-focused, self-doubting, manipulative, vengeful, judgemental, destructive, suspicious, controlling, unforgiving, isolating

New Moon Focus

- *Embrace* the mystery of uncertainty and trust in your inner knowingness to reveal truth
- *Nourish* self-empowerment by substituting supportive sensual behaviours for compulsions or addictions
- *Allow* honest connection with another without sacrificing authenticity
- *Open* to the beauty and diversity of others despite disagreements or feeling misunderstood
- *Be* willing to engage in honest confrontations or difficult emotional encounters no matter how uncomfortable
- *Nurture* innate irresistibility by following your passion to its greatest depths
- *Find* greater fluidity in the relationship to material possessions with appreciation and prudence
- *Allow* your natural sensitivity and perceptiveness to heal and transform self and others

Affirmation: *My vulnerability is a gateway to mystery, magic and connection.*

New Moon Intention

November 15, 2020, 12:07 am ♏ 23°17’

Gemini Full Moon

Reflect on your intention created during the Gemini New Moon, or aspects of your life that highlight Gemini energies:
What's working? What isn't? What can you change?

Higher Expression

Clever, light, alert, lively, articulate, sociable, dexterous, versatile, independent, fluent, expressive, communicative, teacher, writer, presenter, good pattern recognition, adaptable, charming, fascinating, fun, excitable

Gemini Likes: Change, speed, modernity, reading, variety, mental stimulation, being in the know, short trips, quick results, learning, higher education, print media, writing, speaking, teaching, understanding, banter, charming others

Lower Expression

High-strung, restless, superficial, devious, erratic, over-think feelings, stuck in the head, excessive questioning, living from the neck up, short attention span, lacking integrity, manipulative, calculating, unreliable, directionless

Gemini dislikes: solitude, permanence, sameness, solidity, stagnation, dogma, stuckness, reflection, mental inactivity, predictability, being lost for words, ruts, lack of choice, boredom, rigid opinion, being told what to think

Shift:

- ➢ From Superficial to Easygoing by being naturally unique
- ➢ From Insensitive to Straightforward with mindfulness
- ➢ From Anxious to Effective with measured calm

Gemini Moon energy desires to:

♊ ***explore ideas with relish***
♊ ***satisfy curiosity***
♊ ***process feelings through communication***

Full Moon Reflection

November 30, 2020, 4:30 am ♊ 8°37'

Sagittarius New Moon

Element: Fire
Expression: Masculine
Symbol: Archer

KEYWORD: I SEE

Noble Qualities: Adventurous, high ideals, fortunate, truth-seeking, humour, loyalty, benevolence, generosity, openness, freedom-seeking, explorer, visionary, philosopher, forthright, enthusiastic, optimistic, outspoken

Shadow Side: Arrogance, exaggeration, bravado, moral superiority, fanaticism, overindulgence, struggle with intimacy and depth, rude, restless, know it all, tactless, dogmatic, irresponsible

New Moon Focus

- ***Seek*** novel experiences that challenge the body, feed the mind and expand the heart
- ***Cherish*** diversity by nourishing the capacity to see others' points of view
- ***Nurture*** connection without judgement or expectation
- ***Find*** your flow with regular self-care practices that support your whole being
- ***Discover*** ways to make every-day experiences an adventure through humour
- ***Develop*** greater confidence with an attitude of acceptance and optimism
- ***Trade*** overindulgence for generosity by respecting your natural limits
- ***Embrace*** your innate sacredness through connection to higher guidance

Affirmation: *My inner truth shines brightly, always leading me to my sacredness.*

New Moon Intention

December 14, 2020, 11:16 am ♐ 23°07'

Cancer Full Moon

Reflections

Reflect on your intention created during the Cancer New Moon, or aspects of your life that highlight Cancer energies:
What's working? What isn't? What can you change?

Higher Expression

Nurturing, warm, considerate, supportive, familial, protective, trusting, receives care gracefully, emotional closeness, focus on childhood development, distinctly aware of own needs, meet needs with ease, domestic

Cancer likes: Home, children, bodies of water, alone time, internal frame of reference, feelings of belonging, safe and secure home life, financial security, crafting, nurturing new beginnings, cooking, time with close friends, caregiving

Lower Expression

Moody, clingy, needy, oversensitive, self-absorbed, self-pitying, self-sacrificing, weak, sickly, excessive self-protection, feelings of insecurity, overly cautious behaviours, fear of rejection, hiding behind caregiving, defensive

Cancer dislikes: Brutality, aggravation, bad manners, failure, opposition, fake people and things, insolence, interference and advice, carelessness, being uprooted, unkindness, thoughtlessness, neglect, homelessness, disconnection

Shift:

- From Clingy to Caring with easeful support
- From Self-absorbed to Self-reliant with self-acknowledgement
- From Defensive to Receptive with rejuvenation

Cancer Moon energy desires to:

- ***encourage family connection***
- ***create safe, protected spaces***
- ***be in touch with her emotions***

Full Moon Reflection

December 29, 2020, 10:28 pm ♋ 8°53’

Capricorn New Moon

♑

Element: Earth
Expression: Feminine
Symbol: Goat

KEYWORD: I USE

Noble Qualities: Structure, commitment, authority, manifestation, boundaries, groundedness, reserved, patient, stature, prudence, hard-working, cautious, objective, wise elder, conservative, virtuous, serious, responsible, down to earth

Shadow Side: Melancholic, judgemental, overly serious, depressive, fear of failure, resistant to change, alienating, pessimistic, controlling, neglectful, insecure, miserly, sluggish, stubborn, repressive, rigid, materialistic

New Moon Focus

- ***Feed*** your sense of security with small but meaningful acts of self-discipline
- ***Recognize*** extraordinary results come from open-ended process of taking baby steps
- ***Nurture*** generosity while practicing non-attachment to material things
- ***Acknowledge/celebrate*** each accomplishment on your path to success
- ***Nourish*** flexibility and light-heartedness in the face of pessimism
- ***Find*** integrity and dependability amidst the creative chaos of growth and change
- ***Embrace*** your innate need for solitude without excessive self-isolation or alienating others
- ***Receive*** others' admiration and esteem by fostering self-respect

Affirmation: *I manifest my clearest path forward by fully accepting myself, life and others.*

New Moon Intention

January 13, 2021, 12:02 am ♑ 23°13’

Leo Full Moon

Reflections

Reflect on your intention created during the Leo New Moon, or aspects of your life that highlight Leo energies:
What's working? What isn't? What can you change?

Higher Expression

Confident, dignified, fun-loving, flamboyant, likable, affectionate, sincere, charismatic, generous, loyal, performer, hero, generous, abundant energy, benevolent leader, colourful, fun-loving, glorious, artistic flair

Leo likes: Honour, celebration, splendour, passion, being the star attraction, an influential position, charity, children, parties, romantic involvements, privilege and grandeur, personal heart connections, creative expression, play, theatre

Lower Expression

Domineering, pretentious, entitled, stubborn, melodramatic, vain, snobbery, people-pleaser, self-conscious, emotionally overbearing, overly conscious of status, monopolizing attention, self-absorbed, pomposity, pretentiousness

Leo dislikes: Mediocrity, disablement, criticism, meanness, cowardice, intrigue, small-mindedness, deceit, feeling self-conscious, feeling left out, being in second place, lacklustre relationships, being ignored or passed over

Shift:

- from Praise-seeking to Self-confident with self-mastery
- from Self-important to Creative with genuine expression
- from Dramatic to Sincere with generosity

Leo Moon energy desires to:

- ♌ ***shine in unique individuality***
- ♌ ***express talents creatively***
- ♌ ***give with an open heart***

Full Moon Reflection

January 28, 2021, 2:18 pm ♌ 9°05'

Aquarius New Moon

Element: Air
Expression: Masculine
Symbol: Water Bearer

KEYWORD: I KNOW

Noble Qualities: Original, changeable, intuitive, eccentric, innovative, creative, intelligent, perceptive, scientific, humanitarian, idealistic, rebellious, independent, zany, cosmopolitan, inventive, unconventional, authentic

Shadow Side: Radical, detached, restless, bored easily, impersonal, reclusive, non-committal, dogmatic, impulsive, unemotional, stubborn, ideological, aloof,. chaotic, combative

New Moon Focus

- *Consider* challenges from a totally fresh and innovative perspective
- *Nourish* and rejuvenate with a completely new, exotic experience
- *Soften* self-talk and beware of self-criticism while nurturing emotional equanimity
- *Foster* connections beyond your friend group and expand your social circle
- *Encourage* individualism and authenticity by nurturing your unique voice and originality
- *Be* warm-hearted and engaging as you spontaneously reinvent yourself
- *Embrace* your capacity to birth and follow-through with unconventional ideas
- *Free* yourself from others' approval even as you seek to serve the greater good

Affirmation: *At its highest level, my visionary nature supports all of humanity's evolution.*

New Moon Intention

February 11, 2021, 2:08 pm ♒ 23°16’

Virgo Full Moon

Reflections

Reflect on your intention created during the Virgo New Moon, or aspects of your life that highlight Virgo energies:
What's working? What isn't? What can you change?

Higher Expression

Idealistic, industrious, purity of intent, methodical, reliable, health conscious, discriminating, detail-focused, bring order from chaos, earth healer, animal lover, orderly, conscientious, helpful, moved by "divine discontent"

Virgo likes: Meaningful work, accuracy, health and wellness habits, purity, wholesomeness, clarity, diet / exercise plans, structured routines, service, handling details, efficiency and planning, punctuality, discernment

Lower Expression

Sceptical, inflexible, fussy, aloof, perfectionist, over-sensitive, touchy, timid, critical, easily hurt, succumbs to overwhelm, workaholic, excessive detachment, overly analytical, lack of emotional flexibility, petulant, huffy, irritable, frenzied

Virgo dislikes: Disorder, insensitivity, stupidity, quarrelsomeness, unhealthy environments, sordidness, uncertainty, squalor, sloppiness, health hazards, unsafe work space, mess, chaos, confusion, purposelessness

Shift:

- from Worried to Conscientious with devotion
- from Hypersensitive to Tuned-in by embracing diversity
- from Timid to Gentle with worthiness

Virgo Moon energy desires to:

- ♍ ***seek to serve in ideal ways***
- ♍ ***see what is best for the world***
- ♍ ***create order out of chaos***

Full Moon Reflection

February 27, 2021, 3:19 am ♍ 8°57’

Pisces New Moon

Element: Water
Expression: Feminine
Symbol: Fish

KEYWORD: I BELIEVE

Noble Qualities: Imaginative, transcendent , artistic, enlightened, spiritual, unconditionally loving, empathic, impressionable, sensitive, dreamer, visionary, compassionate, dissolves ego, psychic, meditative, gentle

Shadow Side: Delusion, fantasy, disassociation, addiction, confusion, victim, over-sensitive, escapism, spiritual bypassing, overwhelm, fear of shadow, martyr, defeatist attitude, procrastination, emotionally insecure, deception

New Moon Focus

- *Align* heart & soul: support your passions; consistently show-up for yourself
- *Consciously* schedule and fiercely protect your daily quiet time to refresh and renew
- *Foster* the belief that you have whatever it takes to fulfill your dreams
- *Allow* opportunities to get into the flow of creative pursuits and visionary imagination
- *Seek* out practices that help you feel rooted and grounded, and actually do them
- *Journal your dreams:* observe the language of your subconscious at play
- *Accept* imperfections in yourself and others as a natural part of being human
- *Meet* disappointments and delays with light-hearted humour rather than defeatism

Affirmation: *I set clear personal boundaries and also merge with Universal consciousness.*

New Moon Intention

March 13, 2021, 5:23 am ♓ 23°03'

Libra Full Moon

Reflections

Reflect on your intention created during the Libra New Moon, or aspects of your life that highlight Libra energies:
What's working? What isn't? What can you change?

Higher Expression

Sociable, relational, tactful, cooperative, charming, aesthetic sensibility, fairness, idealistic, ambitious, balanced partnerships, good agreements, appreciation of opposite viewpoints, sharing, clear boundaries, interdependence

Libra likes: Cordiality, domestic tranquility, understanding, sharing, finesse, art, good manners, gentleness, harmony, peace, beauty, giving/receiving support, collaboration, cooperation, team identity, sociability, refinement, elegance

Lower Expression

Superficial, judgemental, unkind, crippling indecision, conflict avoidant, people pleasing, insensitive, fear of shadow, loss of self-identity, over-compromise, fear of confrontation, endless aimless debate, fail to take a stand for heart's desire

Libra dislikes: Cruelty, violence, bad manners, awkwardness, injustice, conflict, coarseness, vulgarity, embarrassment, humiliation, feeling outcast, inhospitality, being misjudged, discord, disharmony, disagreements, tactlessness

Shift:

- ➢ from Superficial to Graceful with commitment
- ➢ from Indecisive to Tactful with self-acceptance
- ➢ from Unreliable to Dependable with inner ease

Libra Moon energy desires to:

Ω ***respect & appreciate partners***

Ω ***seek harmony & balance***

Ω ***manifest beauty in the world***

Full Moon Reflection

March 28, 2021, 2:50 am ♎ 8°18'

Aries New Moon

Element: Fire
Expression: Masculine
Symbol: Ram

ESSENCE: I AM

Noble Qualities: Enthusiastic, independent, spontaneous, brave, initiator, confident, passionate, idealistic, leader, enterprising, ambitious, honest, competitive, optimist, assertive, childlike, outgoing, heroic

Shadow Side: Impulsive, irritable, impatient, critical, opinionated, pushy, hasty, selfish, arrogant, brusque, tactless, reactive, resistant, anxious, vain, domineering, high strung, biased, disapproving, unsympathetic, rash, reckless

New Moon Focus

- ***Enjoy*** the benefits of expressing yourself authentically and without pretense
- ***Consider*** starting something brand new that excites and challenges you
- ***Embrace*** opportunities that push you out of your comfort zone
- ***Be*** willing to lead with patience, care, and consideration of others
- ***Support*** yourself fully when you follow your instincts and take big risks for big rewards
- ***Nurture*** confidence, independence and self-reliance while staying open to guidance
- ***Give*** yourself the necessary space and time to develop mastery in any situation
- ***Foster*** the courage needed to soften the natural resistance that accompanies fear of failure

Affirmation: *I have the courage to lead with confidence and humility.*

New Moon Intention

April 11, 2021, 10:32 pm ♈ 22°24’

Scorpio Full Moon

Reflections

♏

Reflect on your intention created during the Scorpio New Moon, or aspects of your life that highlight Scorpio energies:
What's working? What isn't? What can you change?

Higher Expression

Transformative, intense, passionate, charismatic, protective, healing, probing, resourceful, sensual, tenacious, determined, influential, restorative, forgiving, disciplined, subtle awareness of others' motives, seductive, compelling

Scorpio likes: Intimacy, moving experiences, deep emotion, soul-mates, power plays, politics, psychology, persuasion, mystery, investigation, refinement, risk, living on the edge, depth of character, commitment, sexual union, absorption

Lower Expression

Misuse of power, suspicious, obsessive, manipulative, jealous, destructive urges, relentless, insecure, paranoid, underhanded, vengeful, unforgiving, harsh, judgemental, driven by self-doubt, engage in power struggles

Scorpio dislikes: Superficiality, meaningless ties, being controlled, insipidness, dragging things out, authoritarianism, cowardice, frivolity, dependence, shallow relationships, gratuitous flattery, empty excuses, same old stories

Shift:

- from Suspicious to Intuitive with trust
- from Obsessive to Determined by being unattached
- from Manipulative to Influential with personal magic

Scorpio Moon energy desires to:

♏ ***seek intimacy and emotional intensity***
♏ ***merge with meaningful experiences***
♏ ***look beneath the surface***

Full Moon Reflection

April 26, 2021, 11:33 pm ♏ 7°05'

Taurus New Moon

Element: Earth
Expression: Feminine
Symbol: Bull

ESSENCE: I HAVE

Noble Qualities: Calm, stable, reliable, earthy, creative, caring, sensual, kind, pragmatic, determined, healthy, cooperative, patient, financially secure, affluent, trustworthy, security driven, restrained, steady, dignified, dependable

Shadow Side: Procrastination, materialistic, stubborn, rigid, unmotivated, vain, co-dependent, stagnant, stuck, covetous, repressive, overindulgent, inflexible, emotional rigidity, resistance to change, stay too long,

New Moon Focus

- *Foster* innate connection with outdoor beauty and bounty
- *Receive* gifts of sensual pleasure at home: soft textures, harmonious colours, serene sounds
- *Open* to new self-care practices, enjoyable exercise or pampering opportunities
- *Visualize* the fundamental phases of a big dream or long-term intention
- *Embrace* the magic Mother Nature offers in the simple things
- *Consider* creative ways to increase your income or earning power
- *Bring* awareness to deeper personal needs and take steps to nurture them
- *Allow* yourself to view an old situation from a new vantage point

Affirmation: *I am grounded and inspired by my natural connection to planet earth.*

New Moon Intention

May 11, 2021, 3:01 pm ♉ 21°17’

Sagittarius Full Moon

Reflections

Reflect on your intention created during the Sagittarius New Moon, or aspects of your life that highlight Sagittarius energies:
What's working? What isn't? What can you change?

Higher Expression

Freedom-seeking, adventurous, humorous, generous, versatile, open, excellent speaker/teacher, loyal, outspoken, committed to truth, thirsty for knowledge, friendly, outgoing, optimistic, sharing wisdom, exuberant, explorer

Sagittarius likes: Sincerity, honesty, quest for truth, higher guidance, rules and laws, ethics, social standards, finding solutions, justice, foreign travel and people, exploration, freedom, storytelling, excitement, outdoor life

Lower Expression

Unemotional, numb, disconnected, heartless, careless, irresponsible, reckless, self-involved, overly dramatic, self-absorbed, victim mind-set, absent-minded, unreliable, a "Pollyanna", narrow-minded, inflexible, humourless, pessimist

Sagittarius dislikes: Unnaturalness, imitation, monotonous, pettiness, bad manners, unnecessary restrictions, small thinking, pretentiousness, prejudice, pedantry, ignorance, morbid navel-gazing, low/mean attitude or behaviour

Shift:

- from Irresponsible to Engaging with adventure
- from Careless to Concerned by being purposeful
- from Indulgent to Generous through disciplined giving

Sagittarius Moon energy desires to:

- ***seek knowledge and adventure***
- ***delight in pushing boundaries***
- ***share truth in the world***

Full Moon Reflection

May 26, 2021, 7:14 am ♐ 5°25'

Gemini New Moon

Element: Air
Expression: Masculine
Symbol: Twins

ESSENCE: I THINK

Noble Qualities: Communicative, articulate, intelligent, adaptable, alert, clever, curious, fluent, witty, teacher, writer, changeable, analytical, intellectual, good conversationalist, people lover, sociable, lively, charming, versatile

Shadow Side: High-strung, restless, over-think feelings, disconnected, flighty, inconsistent, distracted, scattered, overactive mental processes, nervous, edgy, excessive questioning, superficial, indecisive, uneasy, tense, impatient, gossipy

New Moon Focus

- ***Consider*** a problem or challenge from a variety of perspectives
- ***Enjoy*** the simple pleasure of visiting, socializing or connecting with different people
- ***Explore*** ways to consistently listen for wise guidance or hear others' deeper truths
- ***Gratefully*** receive invitations to speak, present or otherwise share your creative ideas or strategies
- ***Be*** open-minded and curious when encountering people or ideas that feel foreign or strange
- ***Find*** ways to bring calm, organized composure into your day-to-day life
- ***Nurture*** a communications project that includes writing, teaching and/or media appearances
- ***Set*** an intention to open yourself to opportunities for surprise and serendipity

Affirmation: *The sharing of ideas is part of my evolution and brings me joy.*

New Moon Intention

June 10, 2021, 6:54 am ♊ 19°46’

Capricorn Full Moon

Reflections

Reflect on your intention created during the Capricorn New Moon, or aspects of your life that highlight Capricorn energies:
What's working? What isn't? What can you change?

Higher Expression

Responsible, practical, methodical, hard-working, results-focused, cautious, goal oriented, conventional, self-disciplined, ambitious, patient, prudent, mature, strong fundamentals, purposeful, achiever, competent, professional, leader

Capricorn likes: Reliability, to be needed, strong people, good organization, steady structures, clear purpose, firm foundations, social status, being in charge, recognition, traditions, following protocol, respect, responsibility

Lower Expression

Dictatorial, conceited, overly earnest, inhibited, resistant to change, miserly, power-driven, reticent, reserved, uncommunicative, stingy, mistrustful, solemn, unimaginative, overly conservative, grave, stern, severe, inflexible

Capricorn dislikes: Feeling out of control, purposelessness, disgrace, untested strategies, futility, failure, thoughtlessness, vagrancy, ridicule, irrelevance, lack of motivation, humiliation, untrustworthiness, foolishness, inconsiderateness

Shift:

- from Unimaginative to Sensible through humour
- from Enslavement to Dedication with inner direction
- from Insensitive to Sensitive through service

Capricorn Moon energy desires to:

♑ ***focus on the practical***

♑ ***act with measured intent***

♑ ***manifest under controlled conditions***

Full Moon Reflection

June 24, 2021, 2:40 pm ♑ 3°27'

Cancer New Moon

♋

Element: Water
Expression: Feminine
Symbol: Crab

ESSENCE: I FEEL

Noble Qualities: Safety, security, mothering, nurturing, receptive, comforting, emotionally attuned, warm, kind, supportive, helpful, sympathetic, domestic, familial, trusting, caregiver, empathic, imaginative, protective

Shadow Side: Moody, temperamental, sullen, insecure, anxious, needy, fearful, co-dependent, touchy, petulant, self-sacrificing, excessive self-protection, clingy, overly cautious, fear of rejection

New Moon Focus

- *Fully* come home to yourself: honour, nurture and tend to foundational needs
- *Find* ways to feed not only the body, but heart and soul as well
- *Research* creative ways to improve the calm and serenity of your living spaces
- *Reconnect* with family, friends or dear acquaintances not in your immediate circle
- *Easefully* receive love, support and encouragement from others, no matter the source
- *Consider* ways in which you over-give or mother others unnecessarily
- *Open* up to deepen the connection with a close friend or intimate partner
- *Inquire* about ways to support a cause that truly moves you

Affirmation: *Creating a safe space supports me to provide compassionate care to self and others.*

New Moon Intention

July 9, 2021, 9:17 pm ♋ 18°01’

Aquarius Full Moon

Reflections

Reflect on your intention created during the Aquarius New Moon, or aspects of your life that highlight Aquarius energies:
What's working? What isn't? What can you change?

Higher Expression

Intellectual, perceptive, innovative, inventive, independent, rebel, fascinating conversationalist, humanitarian, create community, cosmopolitan, inspirational leader, charismatic pacesetter, operating from larger worldview, clever, inventor

Aquarius likes: Clear thinking, unconventional approaches, future technology, being unique, good surprises, staying cool, solid science, networking, friend groups, fringe pursuits, candour, divination tools, astrology, dreamwork

Lower Expression

Sarcastic, aloof, rebellious, domineering, dogmatic, easily bored, impersonal, non-committal, unemotional, stubborn, combativeness, resist chaos/change, fixed in opinion, difficult to connect with, reclusive

Aquarius dislikes: Being ordinary, routine, pedantry, egoism, stubbornness, stagnancy, stupidity, empty promises, boasting, loneliness, isolation, imitation, dull people, over-emotionalism, disingenuousness

Shift:

- from Impersonal to Impartial through fairness
- from Distant to Accessible through connection
- from Closed to Open with perspective

Aquarius Moon energy desires to:

- ***follow a personal ideology***
- ***be objective in approach***
- ***manifest collaborative communities***

Full Moon Reflection

July 23, 2021, 10:37 pm ♒1°25'

Leo New Moon

Element: Fire
Expression: Masculine
Symbol: Lion

Essence: I Will

Noble Qualities: Vital, confident, romantic, dignified, fun-loving, likable, witty, flamboyant, affectionate, charismatic, magnetic, generous, proud, entertaining, heroic, cheerful, dramatic, playful, warm, creative, glamorous, loyal

Shadow Side: Insecure, self-involved, narcissistic, entitled, self-conscious, other-oriented, shy, prideful, being overly dramatic, self-centeredness, bossy, unnecessarily extravagant, arrogant, self-indulgent

New Moon Focus

- ***Listen*** deeply to your heart's desire and express it to loved ones without attachment
- ***Nurture*** your unique, artistic style with a new or renewed creative pursuit
- ***Trust*** that your open-hearted intentions are received even when unacknowledged
- ***Savour*** opportunities for leisure time and open-ended play
- ***Nourish*** your inner child with patience, kindness and extra self-care
- ***Reach*** out to others to explore activities, games, recreation or romance
- ***Foster*** self-confidence by celebrating small gains or bigger milestones
- ***Take*** responsibility for feeding the fire that fuels your greatest passions

Affirmation: *My unique individuality shines from my fully open heart.*

New Moon Intention

August 8, 2021, 9:50 am ♌ 16°13'

Aquarius Full Moon

Reflections

Reflect on your intention created during the Aquarius New Moon, or aspects of your life that highlight Aquarius energies:
What's working? What isn't? What can you change?

Higher Expression

Intellectual, perceptive, innovative, inventive, independent, rebel, fascinating conversationalist, humanitarian, create community, cosmopolitan, inspirational leader, charismatic pacesetter, operating from larger worldview, clever, inventor

Aquarius likes: Clear thinking, unconventional approaches, future technology, being unique, good surprises, staying cool, solid science, networking, friend groups, fringe pursuits, candor, divination tools, astrology, dreamwork

Lower Expression

Sarcastic, aloof, rebellious, domineering, dogmatic, reclusive, easily bored, impersonal, non-committal, unemotional, stubborn, combativeness, resist chaos/ change, fixed in opinion, difficult to connect with

Aquarius dislikes: Being ordinary, routine, pedantry, egoism, stubbornness, stagnancy, stupidity, empty promises, boasting, loneliness, isolation, imitation, dull people, over-emotionalism, disingenuousness

Shift:

- from Impersonal to Impartial through fairness
- from Distant to Accessible through connection
- from Closed to Open with perspective

Aquarius Moon energy desires to:

- ***follow a personal ideology***
- ***be objective in approach***
- ***manifest collaborative communities***

Full Moon Reflection

August 22, 2021, 8:02 am ♒ 29°36’

Virgo New Moon

Element: Earth
Expression: Feminine
Symbol: Virgin

ESSENCE: I ANALYZE

Noble Qualities: Industrious, idealistic, detail-oriented, organized, home-body, service-oriented, earth healer, animal lover, modest, discreet, practical, humble, helpful, sensible, loyal friend, meticulous, steadfast, devoted

Shadow Side: Critical, worry wart, drama-queen, rescuer, victim, coldness, overly responsible, other-focused, restless, avoidant, controlling, perfectionist, blaming, judgmental, workaholic tendencies, overly analytical, detachment

New Moon Focus

- ***Nurture*** your physical excellence with healthy food, drink, movement and supplement choices
- ***Foster*** routines that constructively support your dreams, desires and intentions
- ***Be*** alert to tendencies of self-criticism and perfectionism
- ***Support*** an attitude of gratitude through accurate self-assessment and appreciation
- ***Allow*** the necessary time and space to ponder and address all the details of a job
- ***Embrace*** order: tidy your space and re-gift objects that may bring others pleasure
- ***Check-in*** to ensure day-to-day responsibilities offer a sense of meaningful accomplishment
- ***Be*** receptive to inner longings and that deeper need for spiritual growth

Affirmation: *Radical self-acceptance enables me to fully serve others and make the world a better place.*

New Moon Intention

September 6, 2021, 8:52 pm ♍ 14°37’

Pisces Full Moon

Reflections

Reflect on your intention created during the Pisces New Moon, or aspects of your life that highlight Pisces energies:
What's working? What isn't? What can you change?

Higher Expression

Compassionate, adaptable, empathic, artistic, humble, devoted, imaginative, intuitive, sensitive, understand all of human experience, visionary, whimsical, a good sense of "the cosmic joke", mystical states, channeling of spiritual power

Pisces likes: Connection, the mystical, good manners, appreciation, to process emotions through dreams, music, poetry, ecstatic bliss states, awareness of subtle energy, inner peace, the ocean, the big dream, spiritual purpose

Lower Expression

Escapist, touchy, impatient, sulky, self-pitying, defeatist, oversensitive, resistant, doubtful, oblivious, distracted, cynical, distrustful, addicted, spiritual bypassing, overwhelmed, panic attacks, dissipates life force energy, dreams life away

Pisces dislikes: Rudeness, greed, the inconsiderate, the literal, the commonplace, criticism, aesthetic starvation, confronting reality, overwhelm, excessive noise, unnecessary interference, cruelty, aggressive behaviours

Shift:

- from Escapist to Mystic by staying unattached
- from Oversensitive to Compassionate with energy management
- from Doubt to Flexibility with determination

Pisces Moon energy desires to:

♓ ***be deeply sensitive***

♓ ***see meaning beyond myself***

♓ ***feel the oneness of life***

Full Moon Reflection

September 20, 2021, 7:55 pm ♓ 28°13'

Libra New Moon

Element: Air
Expression: Masculine
Symbol: Scales

Essence: I Balance

Noble Qualities: balanced, justice, beauty, goodness, fairness, sociability, tact, relatedness, persuasiveness, cooperation, charm, friendly, adaptable, artistic, peaceful, polite, diplomatic, open

Shadow Side: Co-dependent, shallow, vain, indecisive, conflict avoidant, fear of shadow, people-pleasing, critical, judgemental, aloof, unkind, blaming, loss of self identity, aimless, appeasing behaviours

New Moon Focus

- *Nurture* the capacity to negotiate without excessive compromise or concessions
- *Embrace* others' uniqueness and the innate merits of a diverse team
- *Be* honest about wants and needs both as an individual and in a relationship
- *Invite* in greater balance, beauty, harmony and grace
- *Foster* understanding for those that hold opposing views or values
- *Seek* opportunities to develop confidence and encourage self-trust
- *Consider* others' feelings and perspectives when initiating change
- *Support* enduring success by honouring commitments and agreements

Affirmation: *Finding balance with self, life and others makes me a powerful partner with the universe.*

New Moon Intention

October 6, 2021, 7:05 am ♎ 13°24’

Aries Full Moon

♈

Reflections

Reflect on your intention created during the Aries New Moon, or aspects of your life that highlight Aries energies:
What's working? What isn't? What can you change?

Higher Expression

Trail blazer, eager, energetic, enterprising, direct, initiating, spontaneous, brave, adventurous, confident, inspiring, pioneering approaches, ground breaking projects, original, fresh perspective, inventive, assertive, authentic, self-sufficient

Aries likes: Action, leaping forward, spontaneity, the chase, challenges, being first, fast decisions, championing causes, new experiences, leading, honesty, candour, being outspoken, strong opinions, tell it like it is, risk taking, excitement

Lower Expression

Domineering, impatient, impulsive, selfish, argumentative, brusque, arrogant, doubtful of abilities, childish, demanding, harsh, violent, overly competitive, dependency, lacking confidence, self-depricating, egotistical, pushy

Aries dislikes: Cowardice, admitting failure, waiting around, wasted effort, being told what to do, insecurity, no opposition, fluctuation, tyranny, anticlimax, loss, inactivity, sentimentality, dithering, lack of clarity, subtlety, red tape, bureaucracy

Shift:

- ➢ from Impatient to Enthusiastic through relaxed confidence
- ➢ from Insensitive to Straightforward with mindful awareness
- ➢ from Poor Loser to Unbeatable with mastery and self-trust

Aries Moon energy desires to:

♈ ***process emotions quickly***
♈ ***go my own way***
♈ ***seek my own path to truth***

Full Moon Reflection

October 20, 2021, 10:57 am ♈ 27°25'

Scorpio New Moon

Element: Water
Expression: Feminine
Symbol: Scorpion

Essence: I Desire

Noble Qualities: Transcendent, evolutionary, enlightened, magic, passionate, profound, spiritual, sensitive, intuitive, visionary, shamanic, investigative, intimate, surrendering, mysterious, mystical, intense

Shadow Side: Secretive, jealous, paranoid, over-sensitive, relentless, resentful, crisis-focused, self-doubting, manipulative, vengeful, judgemental, destructive, suspicious, controlling, unforgiving, isolating

New Moon Focus

- *Embrace* the mystery of uncertainty and trust in your inner knowingness to reveal truth
- *Nourish* self-empowerment by substituting supportive sensual behaviours for compulsions or addictions
- *Allow* honest connection with another without sacrificing authenticity
- *Open* to the beauty and diversity of others despite disagreements or feeling misunderstood
- *Be* willing to engage in honest confrontations or difficult emotional encounters no matter how uncomfortable
- *Nurture* innate irresistibility by following your passion to its greatest depths
- *Find* greater fluidity in the relationship to material possessions with appreciation and prudence
- *Allow* your natural sensitivity and perceptiveness to heal and transform self and others

Affirmation: *My vulnerability is a gateway to mystery, magic and connection.*

New Moon Intention

November 4, 2021, 5:15 pm ♏ 12°39'

Taurus Full Moon

Reflections

Reflect on your intention created during the Taurus New Moon, or aspects of your life that highlight Taurus energies:
What's working? What isn't? What can you change?

Higher Expression

Stable, affluent, enjoys earthly pleasures, engages creative gifts, contented, great inner strength, financially secure, generous, security minded, appreciates simple physical pleasures, rapport with nature, progressing step-by-step, strong values

Taurus likes: Property, stability, material security, money, sensual experiences, time to consider, natural things, earthly pleasures, quality things, material comforts, beautiful objects, environmental sustainability, possessions, physical senses

Lower Expression

Stubborn, inflexible, obstinate, materialistic, possessive, self-indulgent, jealous, greedy, lethargic, listless, dull, dogmatic, covetous, slave to routine, monotonous, boring, overindulgent

Taurus dislikes: Disruption, being rushed, pompousness, debt, imitations or fake things, fluctuation, rapid change, wastefulness, unnecessary extravagance, letting go, the unknown, borrowing, confusion, excessive indulgence, reckless spending

Shift:

- ➢ from Self-indulgent to Generous with self-care
- ➢ from a Bulldozer to Persistent with appreciation
- ➢ from Stuck to Dependable by releasing attachment

Taurus Moon energy desires to:

♉ ***allow for a natural evolution***
♉ ***develop from the inside out***
♉ ***move to the beat of her own internal rhythm***

Full Moon Reflection

November 19, 2021, 3:59 am ♉ 27°14'

Sagittarius New Moon

Element: Fire
Expression: Masculine
Symbol: Archer

Essence: I See

Noble Qualities: Adventurous, high ideals, fortunate, truth-seeking, humour, loyalty, benevolence, generosity, openness, freedom-seeking, explorer, visionary, philosopher, forthright, enthusiastic, optimistic, outspoken

Shadow Side: Arrogance, exaggeration, bravado, moral superiority, fanaticism, overindulgence, struggle with intimacy and depth, rude, restless, overindulgent know it all, tactless, dogmatic, irresponsible

New Moon Focus

- ***Seek*** novel experiences that challenge the body, feed the mind and expand the heart
- ***Cherish*** diversity by nourishing the capacity to see others' points of view
- ***Nurture*** connection without judgement or expectation
- ***Find*** your flow with regular self-care practices that support your whole being
- ***Discover*** ways to make every-day experiences an adventure through humour
- ***Develop*** greater confidence with an attitude of acceptance and optimism
- ***Trade*** overindulgence for generosity by respecting your natural limits
- ***Embrace*** your innate sacredness through connection to higher guidance

Affirmation: *My inner truth shines brightly, always leading me to my sacredness.*

New Moon Intention

December 4, 2021, 2:44 am ♐ 12°21'

Gemini Full Moon

Reflections

Reflect on your intention created during the Gemini New Moon, or aspects of your life that highlight Gemini energies:

What's working? What isn't? What can you change?

Higher Expression

Clever, light, alert, lively, articulate, sociable, dexterous, versatile, independent, fluent, expressive, communicative, teacher, writer, presenter, speaker, recognize patterns, adaptable, charming, fascinating, fun, excitable

Gemini Likes: Change, speed, modernity, reading, variety, mental stimulation, being in the know, short trips, quick results, learning, higher education, print media, writing, speaking, teaching, understanding, banter, charming others

Lower Expression

High-strung, restless, superficial, devious, erratic, over-think feelings, stuck in the head, excessive questioning, living from the neck up, short attention span, lacking integrity, manipulative, calculating, unreliable, directionless

Gemini dislikes: solitude, permanence, sameness, solidity, stagnation, dogma, stuckness, reflection, mental inactivity, predictability, being lost for words, ruts, lack of choice, boredom, rigid opinion, being told what to think

Shift:

- From Superficial to Easygoing by being naturally unique
- From Insensitive to Straightforward with mindfulness
- From Anxious to Effective with measured calm

Gemini Moon energy desires to:

♊ *explore ideas with relish*
♊ *satisfy curiosity*
♊ *process feelings through communication*

Full Moon Reflection

December 18, 2021, 11:37 pm ♊ 27°28’

The Astrological Houses

The houses determine where the Moon's story will play out in your life. This is where the Moon's energies are brought down to earth so you can address your day-to-day concerns using the thematic energy of each house.

Using your Whole Sign natal chart, find the New or Full Moon sign each month, e.g. New Moon in Taurus. The house that sign is in for you points to the arena of your life most impacted by that particular Moon. Read how the house impacts your monthly New or Full Moon experience on page 18 of this *Journal.*

To obtain a free birth chart go to astro.com

First House
The Self

- Your vitality
- Your sense of self & individuality
- How you stand up for yourself
- What makes you feel unique
- How your world views you
- Health & constitution
- Physical appearance

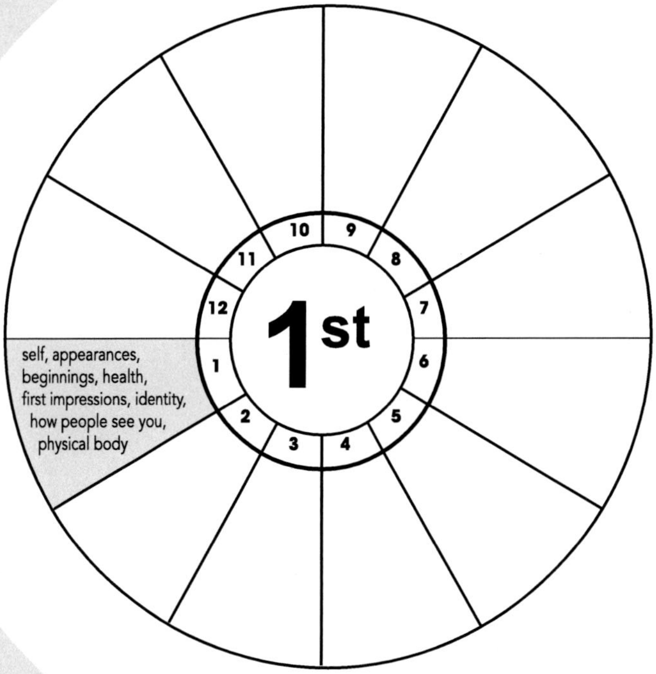

Working with first house concerns

◐ ***Who am I?***

◐ ***What self-image do I project?***

◐ ***Do I trust my instincts?***

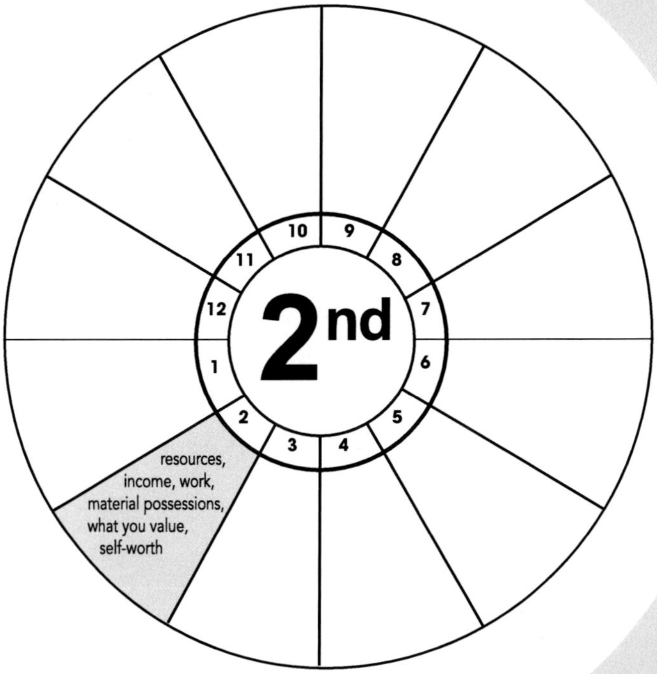

Second House
Your Resources

- Finances & money
- Self-worth & self-esteem
- Your inner resources
- Self-empowerment
- What you value & care about
- Your relationship to money
- Feeling of abundance

Working with second house concerns

◐ ***What do I value?***

◐ ***What makes me feel good about myself?***

◐ ***How does money flow to me?***

Third House
Communication

- Thinking & mental abilities
- Teaching & learning
- Communication
- Information & media
- Your local environment
- Siblings, close relatives
- Short distance travel

Working with third house concerns

◐ ***How do I communicate?***

◐ ***What kind of learner am I?***

◐ ***What is in my comfort zone?***

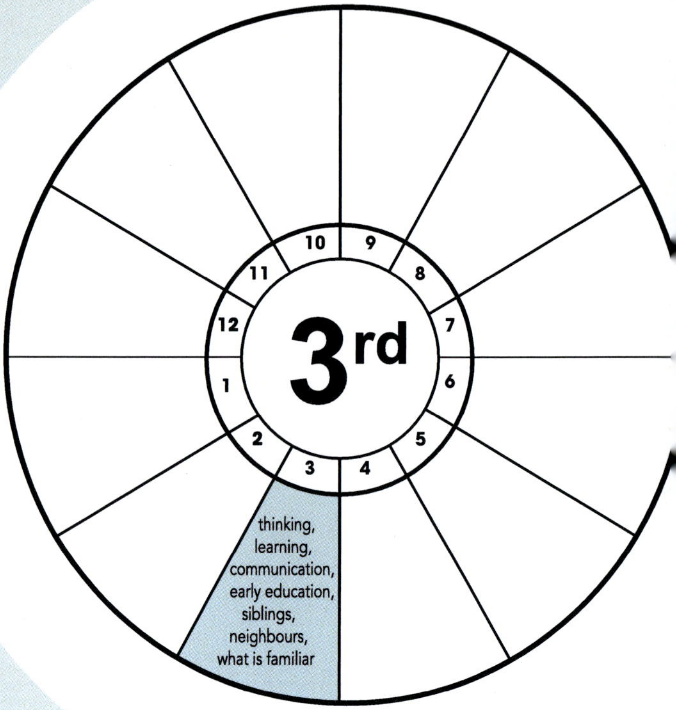

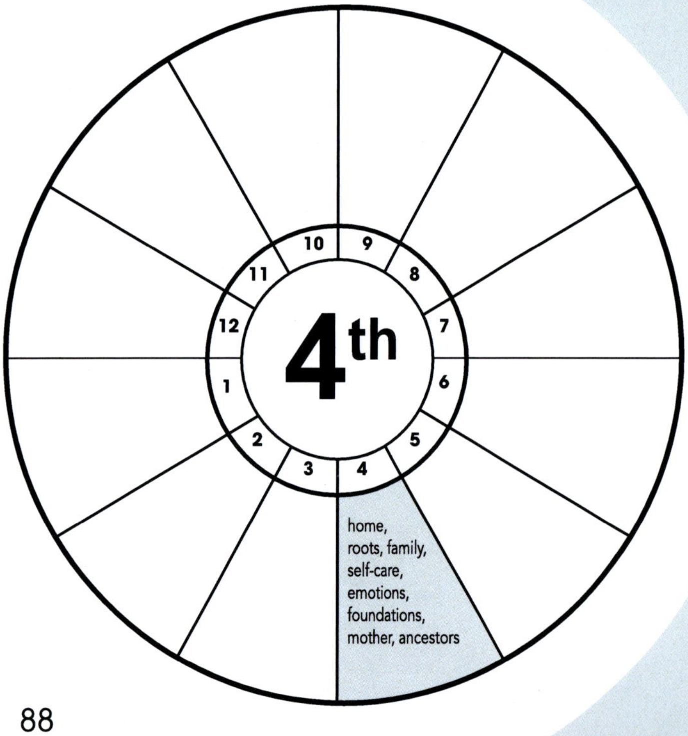

Fourth House
Home

- House & home
- Family & cultural heritage
- Early influences
- Roots & ancestors
- Grounding
- Relationship to your mother
- Self-nurturing

Working with fourth house concerns

◐ ***How do I come home to myself?***

◐ ***What past stories do I tell?***

◐ ***What makes my home supportive?***

Fifth House
Creativity & Fun

- Creative self-expression
- Recreation, sports & games
- Ways to have fun
- Romance & affairs of the heart
- Children & child-like spirit
- Leisure & pleasure
- Risk-taking

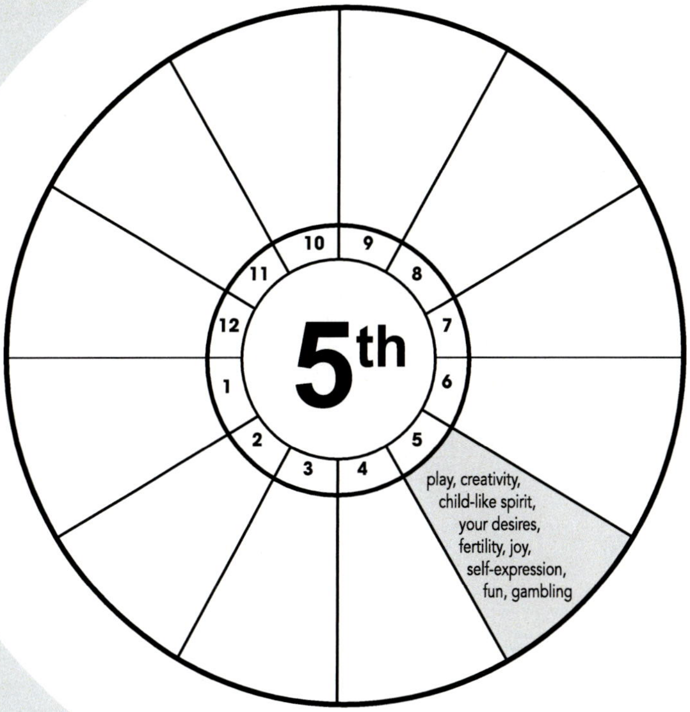

Working with fifth house concerns

- ***What are daily pleasures for me?***
- ***How do I express my creativity?***
- ***What does play look like for me?***

Sixth House
Service & Health

- Duties & responsibilities
- Your health, habits & daily regimes
- Diet & nutrition
- Your day to day work
- Mentoring, being of service
- Co-workers
- Pets & small animals

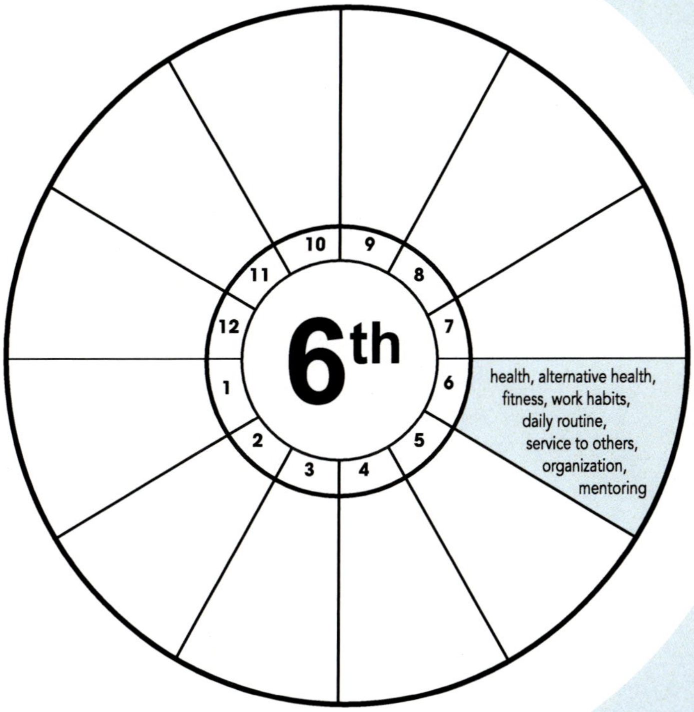

Working with sixth house concerns

- ***How do I fulfill my responsibilities***
- ***What routines support me?***
- ***How can I be of service?***

Seventh House
Partnerships

- Marriage & partnerships
- Close relationships
- Counselling
- Capacity for personal relationships
- Ability to live in balance
- Relationship patterns & lessons
- What opposes you / open enemies

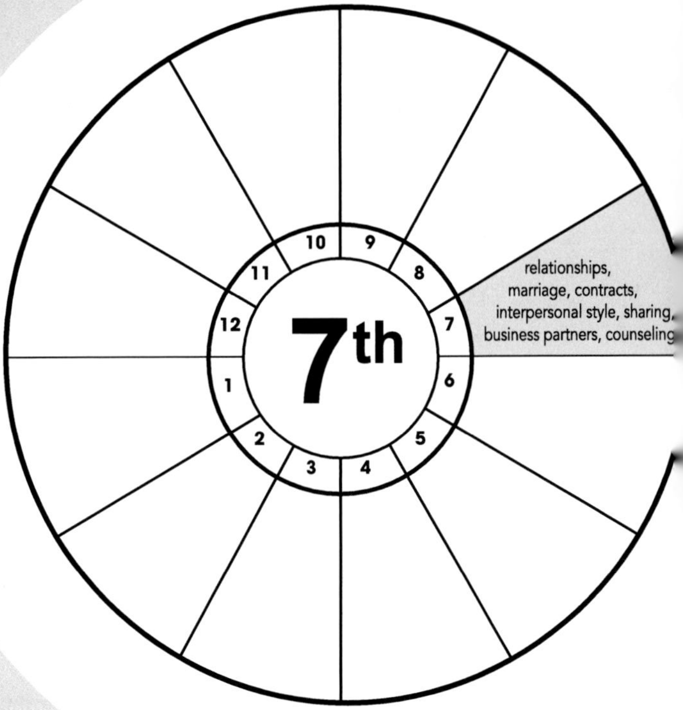

Working with seventh house concerns

◐ ***What does partnership mean to me?***

◐ ***How can I receive love & support?***

◐ ***How do I learn from my relationships?***

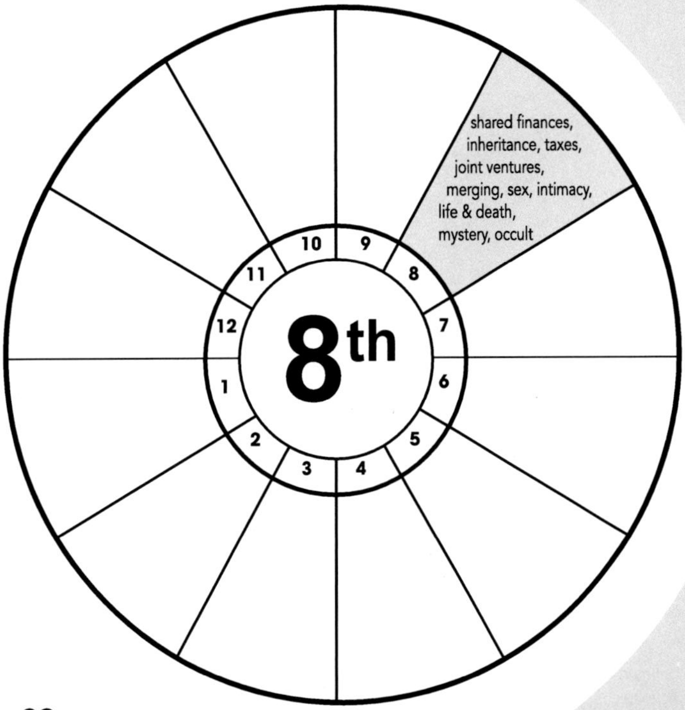

Eighth House
Transformation

- Other people's money
- Inheritances, wills, taxes, debts
- Transformation, rites of passage
- Power & empowerment
- Life, death, sex and rebirth
- Deep fears
- Occult & the mysteries of life

Working with eighth house concerns

◐ ***What is my relationship with other people's money?***

◐ ***How do I relate to my shadow?***

◐ ***What are my opportunities for transformation?***

Ninth House
Expansion

- Higher learning & education
- Your attitudes & beliefs
- Travel & foreign cultures
- Justice, morals & ethics
- Philosophy & religion
- Capacity to be open-minded
- Sharing wisdom

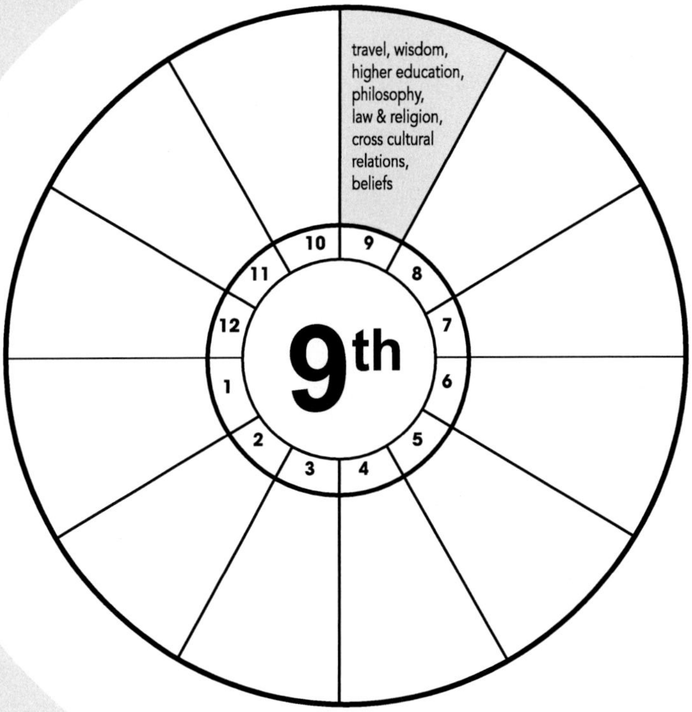

Working with ninth house concerns

◐ ***How do I move out of my comfort zone?***

◐ ***Where do I seek deeper truths?***

◐ ***Am I expanding my philosophies?***

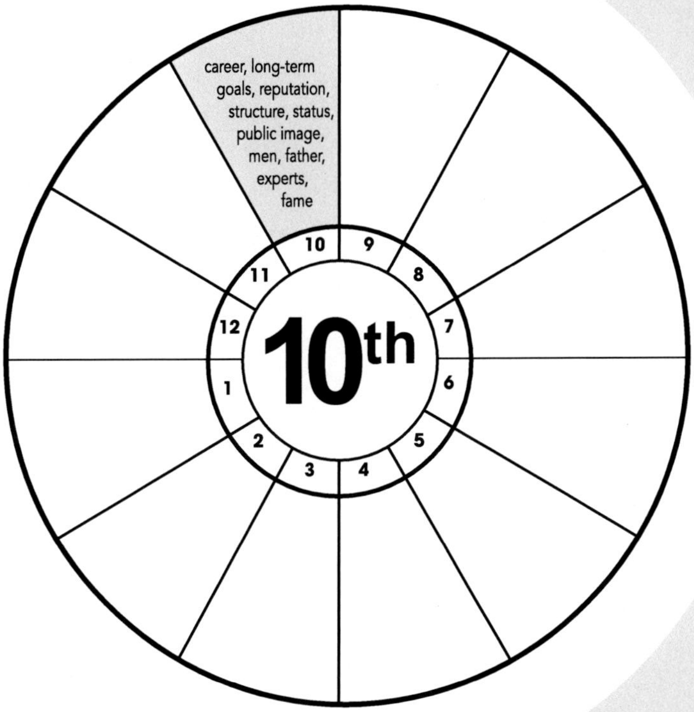

Tenth House
Career & Reputation

- Career & volunteering
- How you are seen in the world
- Your reputation & public image
- Your contribution to the world
- Your relationship to your father
- Your relationship to those in authority

Working with tenth house concerns

◐ ***What is my true calling?***

◐ ***What can I offer my community?***

◐ ***How do I earn respect?***

Eleventh House
Friends & Goals

- Groups & associations
- Friends
- Your supportive community
- How you support others
- People who share your ideals
- Your vision & goals

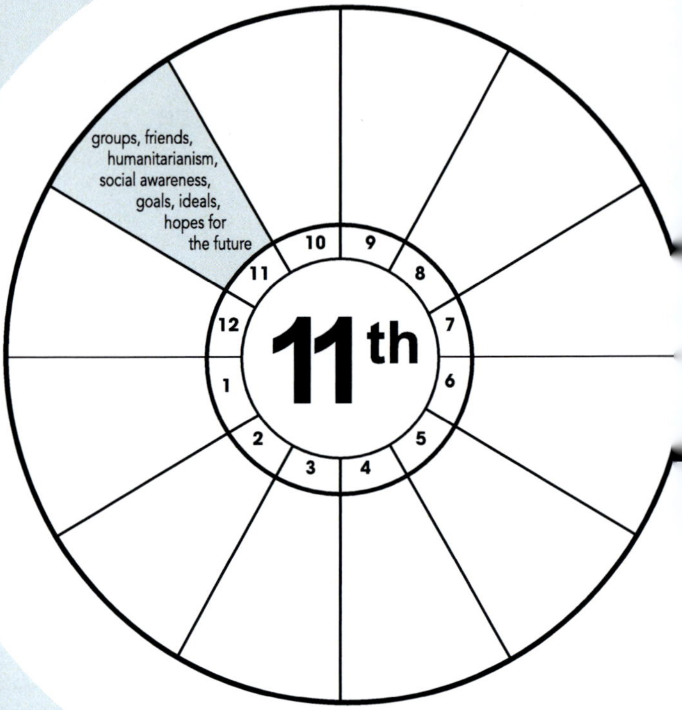

Working with eleventh house concerns

◐ ***Who are my true friends?***

◐ ***How do I work within groups?***

◐ ***What is my personal vision for my life?***

Twelfth House
Transcendence

- Your spiritual life
- What is hidden or unseen
- Your unconscious & deep beliefs
- Past lives & their influence on this life
- Where you retreat or are confined
- Self-sabotage & hidden enemies

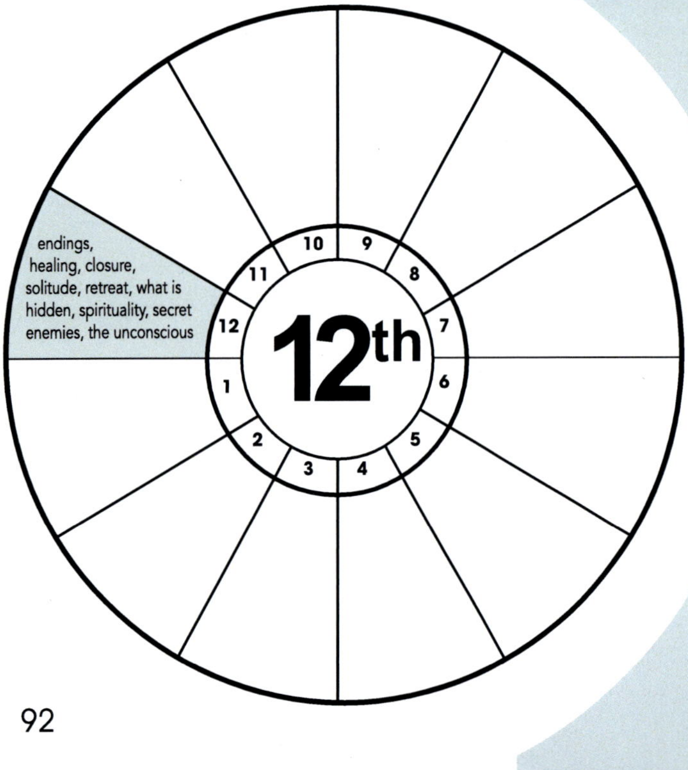

Working with twelfth house concerns

◐ ***Am I willing to explore my subconscious?***

◐ ***How do I undermine myself?***

◐ ***What role does the mystical play in my life?***

House Notes

House Notes

House Notes

Void of Course Moon

Use the Moon's void of course as a timing tool to support your intention-setting practice. Feel her glide through the sky unencumbered by any relationships to other celestial bodies or their energies. This is an ideal time to meditate, dream, imagine, rest or retreat. Read how the void of course Moon may impact your intentions and actions on page 17 of this *Journal*.

NOVEMBER 2020

BEGINS	ENDS	ENTERS NEW SIGN
NOV 1, 9:29 pm Moon trine Saturn	**NOV 2, 4:59 am**	Moon enters Gemini
NOV 4, 8:48 am Moon trine Mercury	**NOV 4, 4:45 pm**	Moon enters Cancer
NOV 6, 8:26 pm Moon square Mercury	**NOV 7, 2:18 am**	Moon enters Leo
NOV 9, 6:05 am Moon sextile Mercury	**NOV 9, 8:30 am**	Moon enters Virgo
NOV 11, 5:58 am Moon trine Saturn	**NOV 11, 11:09 am**	Moon enters Libra
NOV 13, 6:32 am Moon square Saturn	**NOV 13, 11:19 am**	Moon enters Scorpio
NOV 15, 6:12 am Moon sextile Saturn	**NOV 15, 10:47 am**	Moon enters Sagittarius
NOV 17, 2:54 am Moon sextile Venus	**NOV 17, 11:34 am**	Moon enters Capricorn
NOV 19, 11:29 am Moon sextile Sun	**NOV 19, 3:25 pm**	Moon enters Aquarius
NOV 20, 7:49 pm Moon sextile Mars	**NOV 21, 11:06 pm**	Moon enters Pisces
NOV 24, 5:44 am Moon sextile Saturn	**NOV 24, 10:05 am**	Moon enters Aries
NOV 26, 6:46 pm Moon square Saturn	**NOV 26, 10:43 pm**	Moon enters Taurus
NOV 29, 7:48 am Moon trine Saturn	**NOV 29, 11:16 am**	Moon enters Gemini
NOV 30, 11:22 pm Moon square Neptune	**DEC 1, 10:33 pm**	Moon enters Cancer

DECEMBER 2020

BEGINS	ENDS	ENTERS NEW SIGN
DEC 4, 5:29 am Moon opposite Saturn	**DEC 4, 7:53 am**	Moon enters Leo
DEC 5, 5:28 pm Moon trine Mars	**DEC 6, 2:46 pm**	Moon enters Virgo
DEC 8, 5:35 pm Moon trine Saturn	**DEC 8, 7:01 pm**	Moon enters Libra
DEC 10, 7:56 pm Moon square Saturn	**DEC 10, 8:58 pm**	Moon enters Scorpio
DEC 12, 8:58 pm Moon sextile Saturn	**DEC 12, 9:39 pm**	Moon enters Sagittarius
DEC 14, 11:16 am Moon conjunct Sun	**DEC 14, 10:35 pm**	Moon enters Capricorn
DEC 17, 12:34 am Moon conjunct Jupiter	**DEC 17, 1:27 am**	Moon enters Aquarius
DEC 19, 3:45 am Moon sextile Sun	**DEC 19, 7:39 am**	Moon enters Pisces
DEC 21, 5:24 am Moon sextile Pluto	**DEC 21, 5:32 pm**	Moon enters Aries
DEC 23, 5:51 pm Moon conjunct Mars	**DEC 24, 5:55 am**	Moon enters Taurus
DEC 26, 6:32 am Moon trine Pluto	**DEC 26, 6:32 pm**	Moon enters Gemini
DEC 28, 10:01 pm Moon sextile Mars	**DEC 29, 5:28 am**	Moon enters Cancer
DEC 31, 8:45 am Moon square Mars	**DEC 31, 1:58 pm**	Moon enters Leo

JANUARY 2021

BEGINS	ENDS	ENTERS NEW SIGN
JAN 2, 5:00 pm Moon trine Mars	**JAN 2, 8:13 pm**	Moon enters Virgo
JAN 4, 4:34 pm Moon square Venus	**JAN 5, 12:42 am**	Moon enters Libra
JAN 7, 12:54 am Moon sextile Venus	**JAN 7, 3:53 am**	Moon enters Scorpio
JAN 8, 8:58 pm Moon sextile Pluto	**JAN 9, 6:15 am**	Moon enters Sagittarius
JAN 10, 1:29 pm Moon square Neptune	**JAN 11, 8:30 am**	Moon enters Capricorn
JAN 13, 2:22 am Moon conjunct Pluto	**JAN 13, 11:44 am**	Moon enters Aquarius
JAN 14, 4:28 am Moon conjunct Mercury	**JAN 15, 5:17 pm**	Moon enters Pisces
JAN 17, 10:44 pm Moon Sextile Sun	**JAN 18, 2:07 am**	Moon enters Aries
JAN 20, 3:29 am Moon square Pluto	**JAN 20, 1:56 pm**	Moon enters Taurus
JAN 22, 4:28 pm Moon trine Pluto	**JAN 23, 2:43 am**	Moon enters Gemini
JAN 25, 2:17 am Moon trine Mercury	**JAN 25, 1:52 pm**	Moon enters Cancer
JAN 27, 12:55 pm Moon opposite Pluto	**JAN 27, 9:54 pm**	Moon enters Leo
JAN 29, 8:53 pm Moon opposite Mercury	**JAN 30, 3:02 am**	Moon enters Virgo

FEBRUARY 2021

BEGINS	ENDS	ENTERS NEW SIGN
FEB 1, 6:10 am Moon trine Venus	**FEB 1, 6:25 am**	Moon enters Libra
FEB 3, 1:15 am Moon trine Mercury	**FEB 3, 9:14 am**	Moon enters Scorpio
FEB 5, 4:20 am Moon sextile Pluto	**FEB 5, 12:16 pm**	Moon enters Sagittarius
FEB 7, 1:16 am Moon sextile Mercury	**FEB 7, 3:52 pm**	Moon enters Capricorn
FEB 9, 12:22 pm Moon conjunct Pluto	**FEB 9, 8:20 pm**	Moon enters Aquarius
FEB 11, 2:06 pm Moon conjunct Sun	**FEB 12, 2:23 am**	Moon enters Pisces
FEB 14, 2:28 am Moon sextile Pluto	**FEB 14, 10:54 am**	Moon enters Aries
FEB 16, 7:16 pm Moon sextile Sun	**FEB 16, 10:11 pm**	Moon enters Taurus
FEB 19, 2:28 am Moon trine Pluto	**FEB 19, 11:03 am**	Moon enters Gemini
FEB 21, 1:39 pm Moon trine Venus	**FEB 21, 10:53 pm**	Moon enters Cancer
FEB 23, 11:54 pm Moon opposite Pluto	**FEB 24, 7:23 am**	Moon enters Leo
FEB 26, 6:32 am Moon square Mars	**FEB 26, 12:07 pm**	Moon enters Virgo
FEB 28, 10:58 am Moon trine Mars	**FEB 28, 2:17 pm**	Moon enters Libra

MARCH 2021

BEGINS	ENDS	ENTERS NEW SIGN
MAR 2, 9:09 am Moon square Pluto	**MAR 2, 3:38 pm**	Moon enters Scorpio
MAR 4, 11:09 am Moon sextile Pluto	**MAR 4, 5:43 pm**	Moon enters Sagittarius
MAR 6, 4:44 am Moon square Neptune	**MAR 6, 9:20 pm**	Moon enters Capricorn
MAR 8, 7:52 pm Moon conjunct Pluto	**MAR 9, 2:41 am**	Moon enters Aquarius
MAR 10, 10:32 pm Moon conjunct Mercury	**MAR 11, 9:44 am**	Moon enters Pisces
MAR 13, 11:38 am Moon sextile Pluto	**MAR 13, 6:44 pm**	Moon enters Aries
MAR 15, 11:40 pm Moon square Pluto	**MAR 16, 6:56 am**	Moon enters Taurus
MAR 18, 4:40 pm Moon sextile Sun	**MAR 18, 7:47 pm**	Moon enters Gemini
MAR 21, 8:04 am Moon square Venus	**MAR 21, 8:17 am**	Moon enters Cancer
MAR 23, 11:26 am Moon opposite Pluto	**MAR 23, 5:56 pm**	Moon enters Leo
MAR 25, 9:27 am Moon opposite Jupiter	**MAR 25, 11:25 pm**	Moon enters Virgo
MAR 27, 7:48 pm Moon trine Pluto	**MAR 28, 1:22 am**	Moon enters Libra
MAR 29, 8:08 pm Moon square Pluto	**MAR 30, 1:33 am**	Moon enters Scorpio
MAR 31, 8:28 pm Moon sextile Pluto	**APR 1, 1:58 am**	Moon enters Sagittarius

VOID OF COURSE

APRIL 2021

BEGINS	ENDS	ENTERS NEW SIGN
APR 3, 1:23 am Moon square Mercury	**APR 3, 4:13 am**	Moon enters Capricorn
APR 5, 3:05 am Moon conjunct Pluto	**APR 5, 9:03 am**	Moon enters Aquarius
APR 7, 6:05 am Moon conjunct Jupiter	**APR 7, 4:30 pm**	Moon enters Pisces
APR 9, 7:48 pm Moon sextile Pluto	**APR 10, 2:11 am**	Moon enters Aries
APR 12, 8:06 am Moon conjunct Venus	**APR 12, 1:44 pm**	Moon enters Taurus
APR 14, 8:00 pm Moon trine Pluto	**APR 15, 2:35 am**	Moon enters Gemini
APR 17, 11:03 am Moon sextile Sun	**APR 17, 3:25 pm**	Moon enters Cancer
APR 19, 8:03 pm Moon opposite Pluto	**APR 20, 2:10 am**	Moon enters Leo
APR 22, 8:05 am Moon sextile Mars	**APR 22, 9:08 am**	Moon enters Virgo
APR 24, 6:50 am Moon trine Pluto	**APR 24, 12:06 pm**	Moon enters Libra
APR 26, 8:39 am Moon trine Jupiter	**APR 26, 12:18 pm**	Moon enters Scorpio
APR 28, 8:31 am Moon square Jupiter	**APR 28, 11:42 am**	Moon enters Sagittarius
APR 30, 9:26 am Moon sextile Jupiter	**APR 30, 12:16 pm**	Moon enters Capricorn

MAY 2021

BEGINS	ENDS	ENTERS NEW SIGN
MAY 2, 10:38 am Moon trine Mercury	**MAY 2, 3:31 pm**	Moon enters Aquarius
MAY 4, 8:05 pm Moon conjunct Jupiter	**MAY 4, 10:08 pm**	Moon enters Pisces
MAY 7, 3:36 am Moon sextile Venus	**MAY 7, 7:52 am**	Moon enters Aries
MAY 9, 6:50 pm Moon sextile Jupiter	**MAY 9, 7:46 pm**	Moon enters Taurus
MAY 12, 8:23 am Moon square Jupiter	**MAY 12, 8:43 am**	Moon enters Gemini
MAY 14, 6:51 am Moon square Neptune	**MAY 14, 9:30 pm**	Moon enters Cancer
MAY 17, 2:22 am Moon opposite Pluto	**MAY 17, 8:44 am**	Moon enters Leo
MAY 19, 3:12 pm Moon square Sun	**MAY 19. 4:59 pm**	Moon enters Virgo
MAY 21, 3:56 pm Moon trine Pluto	**MAY 21, 9:35 pm**	Moon enters Libra
MAY 23, 5:36 pm Moon square Pluto	**MAY 23, 11:00 pm**	Moon enters Scorpio
MAY 25, 5:19 pm Moon sextile Pluto	**MAY 25, 10:39 pm**	Moon enters Sagittarius
MAY 27, 1:35 pm Moon opposite Mercury	**MAY 27, 10:23 pm**	Moon enters Capricorn
MAY 29, 6:15 pm Moon conjunct Pluto	**MAY 30, 12:04 am**	Moon enters Aquarius

JUNE 2021

BEGINS	ENDS	ENTERS NEW SIGN
JUN 1, 2:13 am Moon trine Venus	**JUN 1, 5:07 am**	Moon enters Pisces
JUN 3, 7:10 am Moon sextile Pluto	**JUN 3, 1:58 pm**	Moon enters Aries
JUN 5, 6:47 pm Moon square Mars	**JUN 6, 1:46 am**	Moon enters Taurus
JUN 8, 11:07 am Moon sextile Mars	**JUN 8, 2:47 pm**	Moon enters Gemini
JUN 10, 1:37 pm Moon square Neptune	**JUN 11, 3:22 am**	Moon enters Cancer
JUN 13, 7:16 am Moon opposite Pluto	**JUN 13, 2:22 pm**	Moon enters Leo
JUN 15, 1:27 pm Moon sextile Sun	**JUN 15, 11:02 pm**	Moon enters Virgo
JUN 17, 11:54 pm Moon square Sun	**JUN 18, 4:53 am**	Moon enters Libra
JUN 20, 6:52 am Moon trine Sun	**JUN 20, 7:58 am**	Moon enters Scorpio
JUN 22, 2:43 am Moon sextile Pluto	**JUN 22, 8:55 am**	Moon enters Sagittarius
JUN 23, 10:09 pm Moon square Neptune	**JUN 24, 9:05 am**	Moon enters Capricorn
JUN 26, 8:49 am Moon opposite Venus	**JUN 26, 10:08 am**	Moon enters Aquarius
JUN 27, 3:07 pm Moon trine Mercury	**JUN 28, 1:51 pm**	Moon enters Pisces
JUN 30, 1:39 pm Moon sextile Pluto	**JUN 30, 9:21 pm**	Moon enters Aries

JULY 2021

BEGINS	ENDS	ENTERS NEW SIGN
JUL 3, 12:15 am Moon square Pluto	**JUL 3, 8:28 am**	Moon enters Taurus
JUL 5, 12:57 pm Moon trine Pluto	**JUL 5, 9:24 pm**	Moon enters Gemini
JUL 8, 12:20 am Moon conjunct Mercury	**JUL 8, 9:51 am**	Moon enters Cancer
JUL 10, 12:10 pm Moon opposite Pluto	**JUL 10, 8:20 pm**	Moon enters Leo
JUL 12, 8:29 am Moon conjunct Mars	**JUL 13, 4:30 am**	Moon enters Virgo
JUL 15, 2:46 am Moon trine Pluto	**JUL 15, 10:31 am**	Moon enters Libra
JUL 17, 7:03 am Moon square Pluto	**JUL 17, 2:38 pm**	Moon enters Scorpio
JUL 19, 12:30 pm Sun trine Moon	**JUL 19, 5:08 pm**	Moon enters Sagittarius
JUL 21, 6:25 pm Moon trine Venus	**JUL 21, 6:36 pm**	Moon enters Capricorn
JUL 23, 12:34 pm Moon conjunct Pluto	**JUL 23, 8:12 pm**	Moon enters Aquarius
JUL 25, 7:13 pm Moon opposite Mars	**JUL 25, 11:30 pm**	Moon enters Pisces
JUL 27, 9:13 pm Moon sextile Pluto	**JUL 28, 5:57 am**	Moon enters Aries
JUL 30, 3:38 pm Moon sextile Jupiter	**JUL 30, 4:08 pm**	Moon enters Taurus

AUGUST 2021

BEGINS	ENDS	ENTERS NEW SIGN
AUG 2, 3:41 am Moon square Jupiter	**AUG 2, 4:46 am**	Moon enters Gemini
AUG 4, 3:38 pm Moon trine Jupiter	**AUG 4, 5:17 pm**	Moon enters Cancer
AUG 6, 6:11 pm Moon opposite Pluto	**AUG 7, 3:31 am**	Moon enters Leo
AUG 9, 8:22 am Moon opposite Jupiter	**AUG 9, 10:55 am**	Moon enters Virgo
AUG 11, 7:21 am Moon trine Pluto	**AUG 11, 4:08 pm**	Moon enters Libra
AUG 13, 4:38 pm Moon trine Jupiter	**AUG 13 8:01 pm**	Moon enters Scorpio
AUG 15, 11:05 pm Moon sextile Venus	**AUG 15, 11:11 pm**	Moon enters Sagittarius
AUG 17, 9:43 pm Moon sextile Jupiter	**AUG 18, 1:58 am**	Moon enters Capricorn
AUG 19, 7:59 pm Moon conjunct Pluto	**AUG 20, 4:49 am**	Moon enters Aquarius
AUG 22, 8:02 am Moon opposite Sun	**AUG 22, 8:42 am**	Moon enters Pisces
AUG 24, 5:12 am Moon sextile Pluto	**AUG 24, 2:57 pm**	Moon enters Aries
AUG 26, 5:14 pm Moon sextile Jupiter	**AUG 27, 12:26 am**	Moon enters Taurus
AUG 29, 10:58 am Moon trine Mercury	**AUG 29, 12:42 pm**	Moon enters Gemini
AUG 31, 4:48 pm Moon trine Jupiter	**SEP 1, 1:26 am**	Moon enters Cancer

SEPTEMBER 2021

BEGINS	ENDS	ENTERS NEW SIGN
SEP 3, 1:37 am Moon opposite Pluto	**SEP 3, 11:58 am**	Moon enters Leo
SEP 5, 10:21 am Moon opposite Jupiter	**SEP 5, 7:05 pm**	Moon enters Virgo
SEP 7, 3:23 pm Moon conjunct Mars	**SEP 7, 11:20 pm**	Moon enters Libra
SEP 10, 12:48 am Moon conjunct Venus	**SEP 10, 2:05 am**	Moon enters Scorpio
SEP 12, 1:33 am Moon sextile Mars	**SEP 12, 4:34 am**	Moon enters Sagittarius
SEP 14, 6:57 am Moon square Mars	**SEP 14, 7:34 am**	Moon enters Capricorn
SEP 16, 1:40 am Moon conjunct Pluto	**SEP 16, 11:23 am**	Moon enters Aquarius
SEP 18, 5:14 am Moon conjunct Jupiter	**SEP 18, 4:22 pm**	Moon enters Pisces
SEP 20, 7:55 pm Moon opposite Sun	**SEP 20, 11:13 pm**	Moon enters Aries
SEP 22, 10:05 pm Moon opposite Mercury	**SEP 23, 8:38 am**	Moon enters Taurus
SEP 25, 9:09 am Moon trine Pluto	**SEP 25, 8:36 pm**	Moon enters Gemini
SEP 28, 12:18 am Moon trine Mercury	**SEP 28, 9:34 am**	Moon enters Cancer
SEP 30, 10:48 am Moon square Mercury	**SEP 30, 8:53 pm**	Moon enters Leo

VOID OF COURSE

OCTOBER 2021

BEGINS	ENDS	ENTERS NEW SIGN
OCT 2, 7:43 pm Moon square Venus	**OCT 3, 4:37 am**	Moon enters Virgo
OCT 5, 4:46 am Moon sextile Venus	**OCT 5, 8:41 am**	Moon enters Libra
OCT 7, 1:03 am Moon square Pluto	**OCT 7, 10:22 am**	Moon enters Scorpio
OCT 9, 2:05 am Moon sextile Pluto	**OCT 9, 11:24 am**	Moon enters Sagittarius
OCT 11, 12:30 am Moon sextile Jupiter	**OCT 11, 1:15 pm**	Moon enters Capricorn
OCT 13, 6:53 am Moon conjunct Pluto	**OCT 13, 4:47 pm**	Moon enters Aquarius
OCT 15, 8:32 am Moon trine Sun	**OCT 15, 10:22 pm**	Moon enters Pisces
OCT 17, 7:24 pm Moon sextile Pluto	**OCT 18, 6:04 am**	Moon enters Aries
OCT 20, 10:57 am Moon opposite Sun	**OCT 20, 3:59 pm**	Moon enters Taurus
OCT 22, 4:35 pm Moon trine Pluto	**OCT 23, 3:57 am**	Moon enters Gemini
OCT 25, 10:11 am Moon trine Mars	**OCT 25, 5:00 pm**	Moon enters Cancer
OCT 28, 2:02 am Moon square Mars	**OCT 28, 5:07 am**	Moon enters Leo
OCT 30, 3:05 am Moon trine Venus	**OCT 30, 2:09 pm**	Moon enters Virgo

NOVEMBER 2021

BEGINS	ENDS	ENTERS NEW SIGN
NOV 1, 1:00 pm Moon square Venus	**NOV 1, 7:11 pm**	Moon enters Libra
NOV 3, 6:32 pm Moon sextile Venus	**NOV 3, 8:52 pm**	Moon enters Scorpio
NOV 5, 12:10 pm Moon sextile Pluto	**NOV 5, 8:52 pm**	Moon enters Sagittarius
NOV 7, 8:44 am Moon sextile Jupiter	**NOV 7, 8:03 pm**	Moon enters Capricorn
NOV 9, 12:51 pm Moon conjunct Pluto	**NOV 9, 10:03 pm**	Moon enters Aquarius
NOV 11, 2:52 pm Moon conjunct Jupiter	**NOV 12, 2:53 am**	Moon enters Pisces
NOV 14, 12:40 am Moon sextile Pluto	**NOV 14, 10:48 am**	Moon enters Aries
NOV 16, 10:51 am Moon square Pluto	**NOV 16, 9:18 pm**	Moon enters Taurus
NOV 19, 3:57 am Moon opposite Sun	**NOV 19, 9:33 am**	Moon enters Gemini
NOV 21, 10:52 am Moon trine Jupiter	**NOV 21, 10:33 pm**	Moon enters Cancer
NOV 24, 12:46 am Moon opposite Pluto	**NOV 24, 10:58 am**	Moon enters Leo
NOV 26, 11:23 am Moon opposite Jupiter	**NOV 26, 9:12 pm**	Moon enters Virgo
NOV 28, 7:02 pm Moon trine Pluto	**NOV 29, 3:55 am**	Moon enters Libra
NOV 30, 11:19 pm Moon trine Jupiter	**DEC 1, 6:55 am**	Moon enters Scorpio

DECEMBER 2021

BEGINS	ENDS	ENTERS NEW SIGN
DEC 3, 12:22 am Moon square Jupiter	**DEC 3, 7:12 am**	Moon enters Sagittarius
DEC 5, 12:08 am Moon sextile Jupiter	**DEC 5, 6:30 am**	Moon enters Capricorn
DEC 6, 11:42 pm Moon sextile Mars	**DEC 7, 6:48 am**	Moon enters Aquarius
DEC 9, 4:59 am Moon square Mars	**DEC 9, 9:53 am**	Moon enters Pisces
DEC 11, 2:40 pm Moon trine Mars	**DEC 11, 4:46 pm**	Moon enters Aries
DEC 13, 9:52 pm Moon sextile Jupiter	**DEC 14 ,3:11 am**	Moon enters Taurus
DEC 16, 11:08 am Moon square Jupiter	**DEC 16, 3:42 pm**	Moon enters Gemini
DEC 19, 1:02 am Moon trine Jupiter	**DEC 19, 4:42 am**	Moon enters Cancer
DEC 21, 9:44 am Moon opposite Venus	**DEC 21, 4:53 pm**	Moon enters Leo
DEC 24, 1:39 am Moon opposite Jupiter	**DEC 24, 3:24 am**	Moon enters Virgo
DEC 26, 3:39 am Moon trine Pluto	**DEC 26, 11:24 am**	Moon enters Libra
DEC 28, 4:10 pm Moon trine Jupiter	**DEC 28, 4:16 pm**	Moon enters Scorpio
DEC 30, 12:10 pm Moon sextile Mercury	**DEC 30, 6:08 pm**	Moon enters Sagittarius

Void of Course Observations

Moon Phases 2021 (Eastern Time)

NOV 8, 2020, 8:46 AM	Last Quarter Moon
NOV 15, 2020, 12:07 AM	**New Moon 23 Scorpio 18**
NOV 21, 2020, 1:45 PM	First Quarter Moon
NOV 30, 2020 , 4:30 AM	**Full Moon 8 Gemini 38** (Penumbral LUNAR Eclipse)
DEC 7, 2020, 7:36 PM	Last Quarter Moon
DEC 14, 2020, 11:16 AM	**New Moon** 23 Sagittarius 08 (Total SOLAR Eclipse)
DEC 21, 2020, 6:41 PM	First Quarter Moon
DEC 29, 2020 10:28 PM	**Full Moon** 8 Cancer 53

2021

JAN 6, 2021 4:37 AM	Last Quarter Moon
JAN 13, 2021 12:00 AM	**New Moon** 23 Capricorn 13
JAN 20, 2021 4:01 PM	First Quarter Moon
JAN 28, 2021 2:16 PM	**Full Moon** 9 Leo 06
FEB 4, 2021 12:37 PM	Last Quarter Moon
FEB 11, 2021 2:06 PM	**New Moon** 23 Aquarius 17
FEB 19, 2021 1:47 PM	First Quarter Moon
FEB 27, 2021 3:17 AM	**Full Moon** 8 Virgo 57
MAR 5, 2021 8:30 PM	Last Quarter Moon
MAR 13, 2021 5:21 AM	New Moon 23 Pisces 04
MAR 21, 2021 10:40 AM	First Quarter Moon
MAR 28, 2021 2:48 PM	Full Moon 8 Libra 18
APR 4, 2021 6:02 AM	Last Quarter Moon
APR 11, 2021 10:31 PM	New Moon 22 Aries 25
APR 20, 2021 2:59 AM	First Quarter Moon
APR 26, 2021 11:31 PM	Full Moon 7 Scorpio 06
MAY 3, 2021 3:50 PM	Last Quarter Moon
MAY 11, 2021 3:00 PM	New Moon 21 Taurus 18

MAY 19, 2021 3:12 PM	First Quarter Moon
MAY 26, 2021 7:14 AM	Full Moon 5 Sagittarius 26 (Total LUNAR Eclipse)
JUN 2, 2021 3:24 AM	Last Quarter Moon
JUN 10, 2021 6:52 AM	New Moon 19 Gemini 47 (Annular SOLAR Eclipse)
JUN 17, 2021 11:54 PM	First Quarter Moon
JUN 24, 2021 2:40 PM	Full Moon 3 Capricorn 28
JUL 1, 2021 5:10 PM	Last Quarter Moon
JUL 9, 2021 9:16 PM	New Moon 18 Cancer 02
JUL 17, 2021 6:10 AM	First Quarter Moon
JUL 23, 2021 10:37 PM	Full Moon 1 Aquarius 26
JUL 31, 2021 9:16 AM	Last Quarter Moon
AUG 8, 2021 9:50 AM	New Moon 16 Leo 14
AUG 15, 2021 11:19 AM	First Quarter Moon
AUG 22, 2021 8:02 AM	Full Moon 29 Aquarius 37
AUG 30, 2021 3:13 AM	Last Quarter Moon
SEP 6, 2021 8:52 PM	New Moon 14 Virgo 38
SEP 13, 2021 4:39 PM	First Quarter Moon
SEP 20, 2021 7:55 PM	Full Moon 28 Pisces 14
SEP 28, 2021 9:57 PM	Last Quarter Moon
OCT 6, 2021 7:05 AM	New Moon 13 Libra 25
OCT 12, 2021 11:25 PM	First Quarter Moon
OCT 20, 2021 10:57 AM	Full Moon 27 Aries 26
OCT 28, 2021 4:05 PM	Last Quarter Moon
NOV 4, 2021 5:14 PM	New Moon 12 Scorpio 40
NOV 11, 2021 7:46 AM	First Quarter Moon
NOV 19, 2021 3:57 AM	Full Moon 27 Taurus 14 (Partial LUNAR Eclipse)
NOV 27, 2021 7:27 AM	Last Quarter Moon
DEC 4, 2021 2:43 AM	New Moon 12 Sagittarius 22 (Total SOLAR Eclipse)
DEC 10, 2021 8:35 PM	First Quarter Moon
DEC 18, 2021 11:35 PM	Full Moon 27 Gemini 29
DEC 26, 2021 9:24 PM	Last Quarter Moon

Synchronicity Notes

Within the scope of intention-setting, you and your heart's desire are at the centre. So, when synchronicity shows up, ask yourself, "Is this meaningful to me?" If the connection touches you, then you are matching your frequency with the universal flow. You are literally synchronizing your own energy with your desired outcome. Where your attention goes, energy flows. Use these pages to help you take note of, track and refer back to your observations, experiences and awarenesses.

Synchronicity Notes

Synchronicity Notes

Synchronicity Notes

About us

Sasha Korper

Teacher / Energy Practitioner / Curious Explorer

As a Certified Mayson Method™ Practitioner, YTT200 Yoga Teacher, Special Education Advocate and Virtues Project Facilitator, I'm uniquely positioned to bring together my two passions: Energy Medicine and Education.

For over 30 years I've trained trainers, developed programs, delivered workshops, and taught classes. My focus is to help you rediscover your soul's genius and clarify your intentions to take inspired action with a joyful heart.

The making of this book has been an expansive collaboration and creative adventure. What a gift it's been for me to share in this transformational project. I trust this journal will support you on your journey into yourself.

Valanne Ridgeway

Astrologer / Channeller / Designer

I am a certified practicing Astrologer (CAAE II), and I channel a higher consciousness that describes itself as a 'soul collective', offering insightful guidance that consistently flows from a place of universal love.

Using my skills I help others see their gifts more clearly and support them in bringing their own light into the world. It feels as though this work has always spoken to the very essence of who I am and what I am here to offer. Over time the accumulation of my soul's experiences has meshed seamlessly with my astrological understanding, intuitive abilities and my passion for assisting others.

I have joyfully used my decades of design training and experience in the creation of this book.

I'm honoured to share my gifts with you in this way.

TOOLS for TRANSFORMATION

We are a growing group of wholistic teacher / practitioners offering you uplifting support in this time of shift, change and human evolution. Through our online community we provide insightful connection, enriching programs, and practical tools as we all navigate our individual and collective transformation.

Join us for our foundational 7-week online course, ***Magnetic Moon Cycles*** — *Crafting Powerful Intentions to Cultivate Inner Clarity and Take Inspired Action*. It's offered a few times each year.

Step into our virtual monthly New Moon Intention Circle: free on Zoom the Wednesday before each New Moon.

ToolsForTransformation.ca

Made in the USA
Monee, IL
13 August 2021

75611832R00064

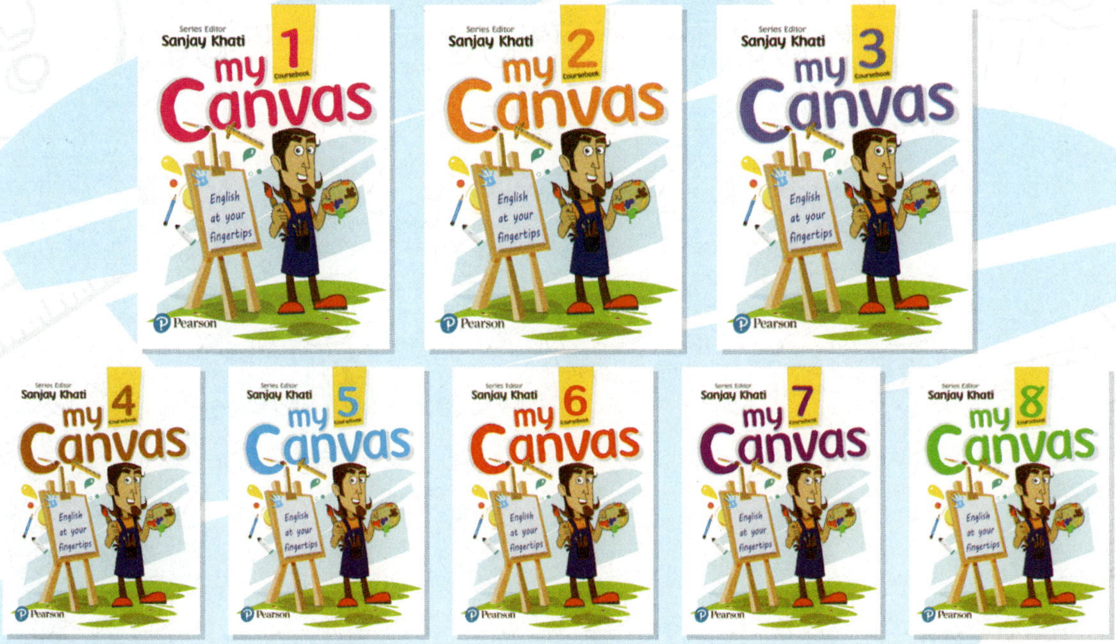

My Canvas is an all-inclusive course in English with a focus on developing skills and building language competencies. A blended learning tool, the course has been designed to teach language for effective communication. The focus on linguistic form and function provides holistic language learning, laying a firm foundation for using English confidently.

The coursebook contains fascinating, contemporary pieces of prose, poetry, essays, articles and drama to enrich the reading experience of young learners. In keeping with the blended approach, for the integrated development of the learner, each book has been divided into many classic and contemporary themes. The pre-theme pages help the learner connect with Multi-skill and MI activities. The Brush Up page reinforces and extends learning with reflection and life skills.

Different aspects of language learning are covered through these features in the coursebook.

- **Comprehension** promotes and assesses literal, inferential, predictive, analytical and evaluative understanding.
- **New Words** helps the learners retain unfamiliar words, phrases and their meaning.
- **Vocabulary** draws the learner's attention to the lexical and semantic wealth of language.
- **Grammar** aids the learners in understanding and applying the nuances of language, grammar and usage through graded and engaging explanations and exercises.
- **Pronunciation** facilitates the learners to master correct pronunciation and intonation.
- **Listening and Speaking** develops oral and aural skills and helps build confidence.
- **Composition** encourages the learner to master writing skills through guided and free writing tasks.

FREE SCHOOL SUPPORT MATERIALS

This book is supplemented by a Teacher's Resource Book and a Teacher's CD-ROM which contain

- E-book with interactivities and audio recordings of the poems, stories, plays, pronunciation drills and listening inputs
- **Animations** and **Worksheets** for use in the classroom
- **Lesson plans** with teaching guidelines for all the lessons
- A **Dynamic Question Bank** that allows teachers to generate question papers for various assessment purposes

For further information, please contact us at **schoolmarketing@pearson.com**.

Tune in to Grammar presents a systematic and step-wise strategy for approaching grammar at any grade. The series presents grammar rules lucidly and leads the learner to assimilate and apply them to communication in everyday life.

The learner is introduced to the concept with a warm-up and led through clearly demarcated stages of acquiring proficiency in grammar. The culmination of a chapter corresponds to the learner being able to use the language in games, projects, activities and a wide range of situations which involve working individually or in groups.

FREE SCHOOL SUPPORT MATERIALS

This book is supplemented by a **Teacher's Resource Book** and a **Teacher's CD-ROM** which contain

- answer keys
- grammar charts
- Teacher's CD with worksheets, animations and grammar games
- step-wise guidelines on how to conduct the Activity in the classroom

For further information, please contact us at **schoolmarketing@pearson.com.**

"In this country Derek O'Brien is synonymous with knowledge based game shows."—*The Times of India*

"There is a bright child in every child and Derek knows exactly how to bring it out."—*Oman Daily*

"Derek O'Brien's new mantra is *Know and Grow*... emphasising on the overall development, life skills and creativity of the child, along with general knowledge." —*The Arab Times, Kuwait*

"Derek O'Brien's way with children is inimitable." —*The Telegraph*

"A great believer in learning-by-doing, Derek O'Brien had set his eyes on general awareness to help students gather information in an interesting way." —*Indian Express*

"Derek O'Brien fills the mind-game with a dash of excitement and fun." —*The Hindu*

Know and Grow with Derek, 3e, is a series aimed at addressing the four vital skills for success in student life—Personality Development, Life Skills, General Knowledge along with Creativity and Thinking Skills. The series can be used as a self-help guide or can be teacher-driven. All useful, everyday information has been classified as KNOW and how to use information to get ahead in life as GROW. The *Know with Derek* and *Grow with Derek* boxes are used throughout the series to highlight different areas of information and growth. The format and design are child-friendly and easily accessible.

KEY FEATURES

- The topics are thematically divided into Units.
- The layout is attractive and student-friendly.
- Colourful pictures and illustrations supplement the textual content effectively.
- The *Know with Derek* section provides interesting trivia on a particular topic.
- The *Grow with Derek* section encourages emotional growth and creativity.
- Quizzes reinforce the learning of important concepts.
- Activity pages engage the learners in stimulating activities.
- Life Skill and Value Education section enhances the positive behaviour in a learner.
- Thinking and Number Skills section enhances the logical and mathematical acumen of learners.
- Fact-based chapters provide detailed information about selected topics.
- Test Papers evaluate the performance of the learners.
- Answer Keys are provided at the end of the book.

FREE SCHOOL SUPPORT MATERIALS

This book is supplemented by a **Teacher's Resource Book** and a **Teacher's CD-ROM** which contain

- **Dynamic Question Bank** enabling teachers to auto-generate question papers, are also provided.
- **E-book:** The e-book has been designed as a dynamic and interactive tool that will make learning more enjoyable. Its various features, such as zoom, highlight and search, aid classroom teaching and enhance understanding of concepts.

For further information, please contact us at **schoolmarketing@pearson.com**.